Living with the Soul

Shree Maa

Devi Mandir Publications

Living with the Soul
First Edition, Copyright©2007
Devi Mandir Publications
5950 State Highway 128,
Napa, CA 94558 USA
Phone and fax: 1-707-966-2802 email:
swamiji@shreemaa.org
www.shreemaa.org

ISBN 1-877795-72-0
Library of Congress Catalog

Living with the Soul
Maa, Shree
Biography, Philosophy, Spirituality, Hindu Saints

Table of Contents

PREFACE

The crowds were immense. It was Shree Maa's first public appearance in India in seven years. Devotees had streamed in from Assam, Bihar and Bengal - the entire northeastern corner of the subcontinent - to catch a glimpse of this small, silent woman. As she stepped onto the stage she seemed more spirit than human, completely serene, and so transparently ego-less it almost felt as if there wasn't anyone there at all.

When Swami Satyananda announced that Shree Maa would begin giving blessings, I started getting nervous. Even in India, a country whose very name is synonymous with holy men and women, the opportunity to receive a personal blessing from a saint of Shree Maa's stature is rare. Sure enough, the crowd began to surge forward like a human tidal wave. I started to panic. Would someone be trampled? Would Maa herself be crushed by the tsunami of people engulfing her?

Shree Maa didn't seem the least disturbed. Sitting quietly on the stage, she closed her eyes and raised her right hand in blessing; the waves of tranquility emanated from her tiny body. It was as if a sea of peace rolled through our hearts. Instantly the crowd became still. One by one for the next several hours, devotees stepped up to Maa, leaving their grief and despair at her feet, and receiving her touch of perfect peace.

In the weeks I spent at Shree Maa's side as we traveled through North India, I never once saw her leave her inner space of luminous stillness. In a world where religious leaders constantly solicit their followers for money, Shree Maa turned away contributions at every stop. ("Give it to the poor.") On a planet where gurus post their own pictures on every pole, Shree Maa shunned publicity and refused to advertise her presence, and still the crowds grew.

She is a living reminder of God in everything and everyone. To the renunciate and the householder, seers both, all of nature and every entity within it was an expression of the pure awareness of the Supreme Being. Everything is holy. As Shree Maa so often says, "Everything is beautiful." Saints like her literally experience divinity in every living thing. It's a state of consciousness most of us can barely imagine.

Though born to a prominent, prosperous family in Assam in the mid-20th century, Shree Maa was absorbed in the life of the spirit from earliest childhood, and enjoyed frequent visions of Ramakrishna. Under his guidance, Maa left home as a teenager to wander in the hills and forests, where she would sit for days in samadhi, the deepest state of contemplative absorption. By her early 20's she was already a living legend, regarded by the Assamese as a human incarnation of the Great Goddess Herself.

I am a professional writer who has struggled on numerous occasions to interview Shree Maa. It was hopeless. She simply isn't interested in talking about herself. She'll just smile, offer a few soft words of advice in the most musical Indian accent I've ever heard, and then signal Swami Satyananda to come over and speak for her - about the Goddess, about the Vedas, about spiritual practice, about how to live efficiently in the world so that we can maximize our time for worship and meditation.

This is the first time Maa has opened up and spoken freely about her life history and inner experiences. This is an amazing document, which describes life from the point of view of enlightenment. It often reads like science fiction. For those of you who haven't had the opportunity to sit with Maa, some of her remarks will sound outrageous, like the most extravagant fairy tales. Others - such as her remarks about projecting her awareness to visit devotees on the other side of the globe - simply sound impossible. Yet those of us who know Maa well can honestly report that she makes these statements as guilelessly and matter-of-factly as a four-year-old describing his first visit to Grandma's house. There is no sense of egotism in her speech. She is simply describing her life as she experiences it from a level of awareness beyond our imagination.

Six years ago my husband was diagnosed with terminal cancer. We were still reeling with shock when the telephone rang. It was Shree Maa. Without warning, she had cut short a tour through India, flown home, and was on her way to our house. It was unbelievable. Maa sat with Jonathan for hours, singing to the Divine Mother and stroking his head. A few days later our doctor called to say that there had been a misdiagnosis. All medical tests had indicated Jonathan had Ewing's sarcoma, but when the doctors looked at him again the nature of the tumor had changed - it would now be easy to treat him successfully. The transformation was so unprecedented in the doctor's experience that the head of the oncology department was considering writing a paper about it for a medical journal.

Shree Maa lives in a different reality from us. But it seems to be a reality more real than ours!

She has quietly been showing us how to love unconditionally and serve selflessly. Maa rarely teaches with words; instead she illustrates eternal wisdom in her actions and in her still, luminescent presence.

Linda Johnson
Author of Daughters of the Goddess,
The Living Saints of India

Oh lovers,
Where are you going?
Who are you looking for?
Your beloved is right here.
She lives in your own
neighborhood.
Her face is veiled,
She hides behind screens
calling for you,
while you search and lose
yourself
in the wilderness and the desert

Cease looking for flowers that
are blooming in the garden of
your own home.
While you go looking for
trinkets,
the treasure house is waiting
for you
in your own being.
There is no need for suffering,
God is here.
- Rumi, 13th century poet-saint

INTRODUCTION

It is a privilege of a lifetime to compile this book using personal interviews given by Shree Maa. These interviews were recorded and carefully transcribed to preserve the narratives and the context of discussions. The chapters are organized by the interviews. In some chapters, material from more than one interview has been combined to present a complete discussion on a specific topic. At the beginning of each chapter is a poem or a context with which the editor captured the essence of her talk. People who have been with Shree Maa for a long time, also contributed to this book with their reflections on this modern day, deeply mystic, saint and how their lives have been transformed through their association with Shree Maa.

I met Shree Maa in January of 1986 in rather casual circumstances. I was looking for a family who would be interested in renting my house in Concord, California. A most unusual family came to see the house: five Caucasian Americans and a slender Bengali lady. I quickly learned that two were gurus and four were their disciples, who wanted to rent the house to establish a temple. I was not sure if I wanted to rent out the house for this purpose and many thoughts crossed my mind, "What kind of temple? What commercial agreements should I negotiate to rent out my house as a temple? What if the tenant-landlord relationship does not work out, how can I ask the temple to move out of my house?" The businessman in me took over and demanded the names of the people who would sign the lease and be responsible for paying the rent. Of course they would have to agree to background and credit checks. I would have to ask for the first and last month's rent in advance. As a first time landlord, my list was long and demanding.

There was no negotiation from the other side; all of my demands were agreed to in the most polite manner. Wow! I was impressed with their simple and accepting nature, but remained skeptical of them. One week after renting the house, I visited the house to check up on my new tenants. The house had been totally transformed - the bathroom floor had new tiles, the rooms were freshly painted, the kitchen was sparklingly clean and my dilapidated garage had been converted into a beautiful temple with a cosmic altar. I was invited to participate in the evening worship ceremony, which I did without understanding or appreciation. Although I was born in a religious Hindu family, I had been minimally participating in Hindu or any other religious practices. In fact, I had not thought much about God. Some thing deep within me wanted to believe in the existence of a Supreme Sovereign Creator of the Universe, but my feeble "intellectual analysis" often led my mind to a very different conclusion - mankind has created God because we are helpless at times and in need of help from a benevolent supreme power.

After a brief stay of six months, the two gurus, Shree Maa and Swamiji along with disciples moved out of the Concord house as Concord City would not allow a temple in a residential zone without a special permit. They moved to a house in Martinez and subsequently, to Napa, their current location, to establish an ashram after staying in Martinez for four years.

As Shree Maa was moving geographically away from me, I was feeling increasingly closer to her in my heart. I would visit Shree Maa once every couple of months for no specific reason. My visit was not motivated by a desire to participate in any worship ceremony or ask her for blessings or ask Swamiji for knowledge - no real purpose at all, except it was like an addiction or infatuation which required a fix. The fix was to be able to see Shree Maa for even a second. Even if I saw her from a distance, I would feel happy for weeks. And then, I would crave to visit again. My wife and daughter, while fully supportive, were unable to comprehend what was happening within me. Frankly, neither did I.

My journey of the last twenty-one years with Shree Maa and Swamiji has been as remarkable as my personal growth. I have walked on this path with their unlimited kindness, grace, pure love, encouragement and teachings, even when my behavior and conduct was not worthy of it. I have often thought of my relationship with Shree Maa similar to a relationship a cracked pot had with a wise Chinese woman. The wise Chinese woman had two large pots, each hung on the ends of a pole, which she carried across her neck. One of the pots had a crack in it while the other pot was perfect and always delivered a full portion of water at the end of the long walk from the stream to the house, the cracked pot arrived only half full.

For a full two years this went on daily, with the woman bringing home only one and a half pots of water. Of course, the perfect pot was proud of its accomplishments. But the poor cracked pot was ashamed of its own imperfection, and miserable that it could only do half of what it had been made to do.

After two years of what it perceived to be bitter failure, it spoke to the woman one day by the stream. "I am ashamed of myself, because these cracks in me cause water to leak out all the way back to your house." The wise woman smiled, "Did you notice that there are flowers on your side of the path, but not on the other pot's side?" "That's because I have always known about your flaws, so I planted flower seeds on your side of the path, and every day while we walk back, you water them. For two years I have been able to pick these beautiful flowers. Without you being just the way you are, there would not be this beauty to grace my path."

Shree Maa is the wise Chinese woman and I am the cracked pot full of flaws. She carries me every day lovingly on her shoulders - always appreciating my efforts, lauding my capacity to retain half the knowledge that she and Swamiji fill me with every week and making me feel that in my own imperfect way I am her instrument to nurture beautiful flowers in this world.

In the end, it's the cracks and flaws I have that make my life with Shree Maa so very interesting and rewarding. I am happy just to be a cracked pot, which is blessed to be with Shree Maa, hopefully forever with her grace.

SHREE MAA'S REALITY

The Chandi is my life.
- Shree Maa

So who is Chandi? Chandi is a name of the Universal Goddess who dwells within all of us - she is the energy of consciousness, she is the source of all knowledge and she is the creator and ultimate destroyer of all thoughts (Chandi's literal meaning is she who tears apart thoughts). The book of Chandi narrates a story of the many battles between the energy of consciousness and millions of demons (delusional thoughts personified by generals and their armies) within us. The battle ends with Chandi being victorious, destroying the forces of evil and establishing the rule of purity in all human beings - making us Gods again.

Shree Maa is a living testament to Chandi fulfilling her promise to transform all humans into Gods and Goddesses. Shree Maa is completely devoid of thoughts we are so familiar with: anger, passion, desire, self-conceit, self-deprecation, ego, etc. Even a casual visitor can sense Chandi brilliantly shining within Shree Maa with all her weapons: energies of concentration, courage, knowledge, purity, devotion, and sacrifice.

The following is an excerpt from the Chandi. This excerpt begins when two servants of Self-Conceit and Self-Deprecation, whose names are Passion and Anger, become aware of the soul's inherent divine illumination and beauty. They rushed to Self Conceit and told him about the incomparable beauty of the Goddess. Self-Conceit, being true to his nature, immediately wanted to own HER, and sent a thought, Flattery, as an ambassador to bring HER to him.

The Ambassador said: "Oh Energy of Supreme Consciousness, all of humanity has been defeated by Self Conceit, and obeys his commands. No one can violate his order. He has sent a very attractive proposal. 'Oh Goddess, we consider you to be the ultimate jewel of all energies in the creation; therefore come to us because you deserve to be with us. Come and serve me and my extremely valiant brother, Self-Deprecation.'"

The Goddess replied: "Whoever will defeat me in the battle, whoever will lose his self-conceit in me, whoever will see all the force of the universe as one within me, he will be my master. So return to the great thoughts Self-Conceit and Self-Deprecation. When they conquer me, I will marry."

As the story unfolds in Chandi, the Goddess destroys many other pernicious thoughts in battles including Sinful Eyes, Passion, Anger, Desire and ultimately defeats Self-Conceit and Self-Deprecation. With all our thoughts becoming silent, our consciousness realizes the bliss of union with our true nature - a state of total peace and harmony. We become divine again.

The main mantra of the Chandi, "Om Aim Hrim Klim Chamundayai Viche," reminds us that our mind's perception is really a reflection and interplay of our own three natures (Satva, Rajas, Tamas). The sum total of all perceptions becomes one's reality of this universe. It is similar to the Christian doctrine that God manifests himself in the world; the Buddhist would say the thought Nirvana and Prakriti are identical; and Sufi master Ibn Arabi would say the same thing, every thing belongs to Him, stems from Him and moves towards Him. His illumination is so powerful that it exceeds our capabilities of perception, and we can only recognize his creation, which disguises Him.

Shree Maa often says He is inside you, He is outside you and He is you - nothing exists except GOD. GOD and his creation - the one and the many, the unmanifest and the manifest, the content and the form, the metaphysical and the physical - it is the relationship between a center and a form. The center, a point, has no dimension or perceivable form; yet all forms, including a circle and a globe are born from it. The law of the circle or globe is constant movement, while the law of the center is peace. For humans to perceive the center, which belongs to another dimensional order, the center must manifest as a circle with movements (in Shree Maa's words a form with energy) for us to perceive. Behind every movement is a wish for change; yet we often wish that forms and relationships would not change, but rather stay as they are. Since the nature of the Nature is to change, practically we have only two options: 1) to simply be a witness to this drama with love and detachment; and/or 2) to move towards the center. Only by reaching the center, can we become free from change.

So possibly the greatest purpose of Shree Maa's life is to remind us to step out of the melodrama, become the witness and move towards/into the center. Shree Maa has allowed us to witness her life to inspire us to do just that. Nothing less and nothing more - just be with the center in total peace and harmony.

Shree Maa's communication style is so frank and revealing and she speaks English so well, that she gives an unusually insightful view into the enlightened state. Her perspective comes from a paradigm outside our reality, yet having lived in this country for many years, she understands the western reader's unique dilemma, and is able to give us a glimpse into her world.

For those of you who are familiar with the lives of other saints, Shree Maa's story will seem familiar. If you are new to metaphysical studies, you might find the ultimate reality is stranger than fiction. You may be unsure if these are true stories or fairly tales. Each one of us will approach reading this book with our unique perspective ranging from curious to disbelief. Please try to keep an open mind as the rewards could be beyond your imagination; it may just totally transform your entire life.

This book is about Shree Maa's life and how her life has transformed us just by being around her. We have known Shree Maa for a very long time and most of us have gone through the same transformational journey: from wanting to believe, but not sure if God exists - to becoming absolutely sure that nothing else exists but God. One of the reasons Shree Maa is sharing her story is to remind us that we all can have the same magical relationship with God that she has. The stories that follow will illustrate what could be in store for each of us in the near or distant future.

> *Someone inside of us is now kissing the hand of God,*
> *and wants to share with us that grand news.*
> *- Hafiz*

EARLY YEARS

Every human being can realize
That it's not hard to know SELF,
It's not a miracle.
These stories are not miracles at all.
- Shree Maa

It is a mystery why the infinite and formless SELF embodies himself (or herself) in a finite form and acts as a human. Sri Ramakrishna explained this mystery over a century ago, "(S)he who liberates others is an embodiment of God. These high souls return from total liberation to the world for the welfare of humanity." Their births, life styles, actions and behaviors are inscrutable to humans. They have love and compassion for all - the good, the bad, the pious, the sinful, the destitute and the divine. They keep their minds both on an absolute plane of existence and on the relative existence of the world.

During this interview, Shree Maa tells us about her birth in her present form. As the interview began, a bright ray of sunlight came out of the woods through the window behind her, and reflected off Shree Maa's head, so that the light sprayed in many different directions. It was quite an interesting sight. At one point in the interview the light completely obscured her face from our view. It was one of those moments of inspired serendipity.

Shree Maa:

My mother got married when she was fourteen years old and when she was two month's pregnant with me, my father and mother went to visit the Kamakhya Temple. At that time there was no way to go to the temple by car, so you had to walk to get there.

When they finally reached the temple and walked up the steps to the top, a respected saint named Bhuvananda Swami was standing there. He said, "I knew you both were coming today. I've been waiting for you for a long time. I want to share some blessings with you. First, come to my ashram, and after that you can visit the temple."

The saint told my mother, "I will initiate you with a special mantra, because a higher soul is coming to you." He gave my mother initiation and told her, "You have to do lots of work to purify yourself. When she is born, please bring her to me, and when she will be two months old, bring her back again."

So when I was born, my parents took me to see him. The Guru initiated my mom again, and he also initiated me. When he gave initiation to my mom, she levitated above the ground. Her third eye was glowing and was as large as a ping pong ball. She had a hard time coming back down to normal consciousness, and the Guru was a little afraid, so he started reciting mantras until she came back to the ground.

Shree Maa's mother - Bara Maa

ACTING LIKE A HUMAN

When we take a human birth, we have to act like a human. Krishna's parents knew their child would be an incarnation of God. But when Krishna was born, his parents treated him like a normal child, even though they knew he was divine. This is the illusion of maya (the illusion that the material world is the only reality and we are separate from God).

That's also the way I grew up. My mother prayed for a great child, so a soul came. When my mom was pregnant with me, she was united with divine consciousness and everyone could see she was radiant. After I was born, maya caught her because she was so involved in raising her other children that she forgot about God. That is human life.

When Ramakrishna was coming into this world, his mother and father knew who he was, but when he was born they forgot. They started to take care of him like he was a normal child. God is tricky that way. These parents needed to forget; otherwise they couldn't have raised their children.

Shree Maa with her cousin sisters

MY FAMILY

After my birth, my mother became pregnant again. My father was the manager of a British tea garden located outside a small village where there was no hospital or school. There was nothing around the tea estate. It was an isolated area outside the village. Therefore, my Grandma took care of me. My mother came occasionally from the tea gardens to Grandma's house to visit me, but I grew up with my Grandma.

I can't tell you too much about my parents, because I never lived with them, but I know my father was a little crazy. He was both worldly and spiritual. The story I heard was that he was not perfect for the world or for spirituality. My father's great grandfather was a famous sage and my uncle renounced the world and became a sadhu, but I had little relationship with my father's family or with my father and mother.

One good thing about my childhood was that I was always detached. Usually a child cries for her parents, but I didn't.

My uncle and Grandma never liked to send me to my mom's house because it was empty, and they were attached to me. I was attached to Grandma somewhat, because she took care of me. Her teaching was very strong and perfect, but her family didn't understand who she was. Even though she took care of the whole family, she always kept her prayers and I learned that discipline from her.

Grandma's dedication to spiritual practice and her efficiency was amazing. I watched how she did everything. Her main teaching was to live with God and love God all the time. Even though she experienced many difficulties in her life, she demonstrated that if you love God, God will love you back.

Shree Maa's Grandma - Didi Maa

KRISHNA LIGHTS UP THE NIGHT

I slept with Grandma in the meditation room and sometimes, in the middle of the night, I saw a light come from the Krishna statue on the altar. I'd say, "Grandma, a light is coming from Krishna!" And she'd say, "It's nothing." She never made a big deal of my experiences.

For instance, during my childhood there was a big light on my left side and behind me. We lived near a jungle and there was hardly any light. But when I walked in the dark, a big light would light my path so I could see. This light was with me all the time.

So many times I told her, "Grandma, a big light is walking with me. Maybe it's a ghost!"

Grandma would say, "Don't be afraid, God is protecting you."

Grandma was always with her Guru, Ramakrishna. She would tell me, "If you need anything talk with Ramakrishna." She taught me to do puja in the morning and evening starting when I was very young. My uncle later told me that my first Guru was my Grandma. If my Grandma hadn't been my Guru, I don't know if I could have gotten everything. She made my consciousness go towards God all the time. Grandma and me; perfect environment for growing up in a divine way.

Grandma, Shree Maa and her cousin sisters

GRANDMA'S DEVOTION

My Grandma demonstrated that if you act efficiently, you will get a positive result. For example, when she cooked, she chanted "Om Hrim Annapurnayai Namah," (this is a mantra for Annapurna, the Goddess of food and nourishment). When she cooked, she saved a little food: dal and rice and oil, in another container with Annapurna's name. First she gave to Annapurna, then she cooked for us.

She used all the food in that container for an annual festival when she fed everybody. She also had a little pot for Lakshmi on her altar, and everyday she put in a coin to save. She used all those coins for a big festival, when she bought something special for us all.

My mother and all her brothers had lived together under the joint family system. For a few years I lived with my elder uncle, who was an engineer for a British oil company. He had four kids. We were all kind of the same age, and we grew up together. When he had to move from his house to the company's house, he wanted to take me with him. But my Grandma said, "If you take her, I'll cut your hand!" That was a great blessing because after that I lived with Grandma - just Grandma and me were the only two women of the house.

Grandpa died a long time ago. Grandma had seven sons, and one daughter - my mom. When Grandma's youngest son was six months old, Grandpa died of a tumor inside his ear. My elder uncle, my Grandma's eldest son, was fourteen years old. He was going to study to be a doctor, but when Grandpa died, he had to work to take care of the whole family. The British officers loved him because he was so intelligent, so they helped him study, and he became an engineer. After that, all my uncles got into good professions. My second uncle was an executive engineer, my third uncle was an electrical engineer, the fourth was a construction supervisor, the fifth was an accountant, the sixth was a very successful businessman, and the seventh became a Professor in business management.

KALI EATS THE OFFERING

We had lots of banana trees, and when the bananas were ripe, they were kept inside the temple. (Laughing) You know, nobody would steal from the temple. One day, when I was four years old, I was giving banana prasad (offering of food) to a picture of Kali and I was crying, "Kali! Eat, eat! Everybody says you are a Goddess! Why don't you eat this banana!" You wouldn't believe it, but Kali appeared and ate the whole banana! The tongue came out of the picture and ate the banana.

Yes. (Laughing) Isn't that something? (At that time) I thought it was normal. So I told Grandma, "Kali ate a banana today!" But Grandma didn't make anything out of it. She didn't give any importance to my experiences, so I didn't give any importance to them either. Through that relationship I learned detachment. I think that helped me become strong and quiet inside. (Laughing) Either she didn't believe me or she was teaching me. I felt it was a teaching. Sometimes I told Grandma that Ramakrishna said this or that to me, and she would completely avoid any conversation about it. She wouldn't say anything.

For a reader, inexperienced in mysticism, these stories may appear hard to believe and in fact may come across as pure fantasy. The importance of this episode lies in the fact that Shree Maa established personal relationships with Kali and Ramakrishna very early in her life, and these relationships have guided all her actions in her life. Every action she performs is for the welfare of humanity without even a trace of fleeting selfish thoughts.

RAMAKRISHNA SPEAKS

Once Thakur (an affectionate name for Ramakrishna) told me, "I will be with you all the time, but you must keep this secret. Someday the time will come to tell others, but now keep everything secret, because if you don't, I will leave you." I always kept this vow.

I have talked with him all the time, ever since my childhood. Sometimes I sit down at my altar to talk and sometimes he comes in dreams. But I can talk to him anywhere, at any time. When I was young, I sometimes hid so I could talk with God.

The first time I heard Ramakrishna was when I was four years old and he said to me, "Oh, you came again. Much more needs to be done in this Age of Darkness (Kali Yuga). You've got to show what divine life means and what spiritual practice and sacrifice are."

Later that year, I was sweeping the house and when I was finished, I threw the broom in to the corner where it was kept. Suddenly, I heard Ramakrishna's voice. When he talked with me he would say "Hega," which means "Hello," in Bengali. He said, "Hega, why are you throwing that broom? It cleans your floor. Cleanliness is next to Godliness. You should respect your actions all the time." So I bowed down to the broom. He was teaching me to honor and respect everything.

Thakur told me, "Family relationship has attachment - 'I' and 'mine'. If you try to keep your blood connections, you will fall down from God. Therefore, you have to be careful. Just go forward. Otherwise, you can get caught in illusion. Don't look backward." Yes, the time has come (to share with readers her conversations with Ramakrishna).

While we are talking about my childhood home, I want to tell you a story about how the Kamakhya temple[1] was built.

Kamakhya Temple, Gauhati

---

1 The Story of Kamakhya is included in the reference section at the end of the book

RELIGIONS - IT IS THE SAME TRUTH, THE SAME WISDOM

He left His fingerprint on a glass the earth drinks from.
Every religion has studied it.
Churches and temples use the geometry of those lines
To establish rites and laws and prayers,
And our ideas of the universe.
I guess there is no telling how out of hand
And wonderfully wild things will get
When our lips catch up to His.
-Mira Bai

Faith lights the path for a soul, fills the journey with joy, ultimately guiding it to its destination. All faiths lead to same destination - center, the center of total peace and harmony. It is less important which path one chooses, what counts, are one's commitment, courage, dedication and efforts to progress toward the destination. Having reached the center, Shree Maa's journey is complete. She is a living testament of what one becomes when (s)he reaches the center, one's outlook on the universe and one's purpose in life. For the rest of us who are works in progress, she provides us a role model, encouragement and helping hands in our journey.

This interview took place a week before Christmas. Shree Maa celebrates this holiday with Christmas carols, prayers to Jesus, and even a Christmas tree. A sculpture of Jesus that Shree Maa made with her own hands is decorated with flowers and red and blue Christmas lights. Shree Maa began this conversation by talking about Jesus.

Shree Maa:

Thakur taught me that if I respect everything all the time, he will be with me. He was always with me during my childhood and then Jesus came. I was in the fourth grade.

Jesus would always play with me. That was so much fun. He would talk about his life and about how he was born. He told me many stories. Before he came to me, I wasn't interested in Christianity or Judaism. I knew he was a saint and that Western people prayed to him, but I knew nothing about Christianity.

Jesus told me that when he was seven, he met a king who had come from Jaipur, India, for business. When the king saw Jesus, he fell in love with him and wanted him to come to India. Jesus's heart was bubbling to go, but Mary wouldn't let him.

After a couple of years the king came again. He said, "This boy is special. I would like to take him with me. It would be good for him to go to India, because he will learn many things there." At that time Jesus was ready and he went with the king. Jesus said he felt at home in India and the king introduced him to many people and places.

Then Jesus started to travel by himself. He was bright, interested and learned quickly. He fell in love with Sanskrit and Ayurvedic medicine. He learned from Brahmin pundits in Benares and sometimes he defeated them in debate. A couple of Brahmin pundits felt he was someone very special, but they still wanted him to go back to his own country.

(Laughing) Jesus had a little bit of a hot temper. It was his intolerance of ignorance and duality. That's the same temper that caused him to turn over the moneylenders' tables in the temple in Jerusalem.

He learned pure knowledge, but he did not perform sadhana (spiritual practices). One pundit from Benares told Jesus that he should leave or the other pundits would beat him and may even kill him.

One pundit took him far away to another village. I don't know how true this is, it's just what he told me. In that village, everyone was so happy to see him. They felt that God had come from heaven. He did a lot of seva (service), cured people with his Ayurvedic medicine and shared his knowledge. He became well known and his name started to spread. Then the Brahmins in that village said he should leave. They told him he should go back to his own country because he was ruining their reputations. Again he was told he might be killed, so eventually he went home.

When he came back, his family neglected him. His brothers teased him because he was different. Then he left home and started wandering again. He didn't talk about when he realized who he was. So Jesus came to me in that way and the Jesus story is not finished. From that time on, I worshipped Jesus as well as Ramakrishna. Jesus said to me many times, "One day I will come to you. I haven't fulfilled my desires in India, so I must finish that task. One day I will study Sanskrit and the Vedas in even greater depth".

SPENDING TIME WITH BUDDHA

From the sixth to the eighth grade I was with Buddha. Every day we had forty-five minutes off from school and during that time I sat in a Buddhist temple and joined in every ceremony. That was one of the reasons why I was not a very good student. After school I would visit with a Buddhist family and learn their rituals and culture.

When you are born, you have some human tendencies. But, if an enlightened teacher is with you all the time telling you stories, then your mind will stay focused on God. So I had a companion all the time. I thought this was normal.

From the ninth to the eleventh grades I studied the Muslim religion. Our neighbor was a Muslim, and I was so impressed that he got up every morning at four o'clock to pray, that I started to meditate in the Muslim way. While my neighbors read their Koran early in the morning, I would sit down with them and meditate.

I never felt that the Muslims were of a different religion. It felt that we were all human beings and we just pray in different ways. Also in Hinduism, I never made distinctions between Krishna and Shiva and Shakti.

God is God. (Laughing) When our Muslim neighbors prayed, we joined with them and they joined with us when we prayed. We were very close; we were one family.

I totally followed what Ramakrishna did. He was guiding me. It doesn't matter who the teacher is, Buddha, Jesus or Ramakrishna. It's the same truth, the same wisdom.

Shree Maa as a young student

VISIONS

I had to seek the Physician because of
The pain this world caused me.
I could not believe what happened when I got there,
I found my Teacher.
Before I left, he said,
"Up for a little homework, yet?"
"Okay," I replied.
"Well then, try thanking all the people
Who have caused you pain.
They helped you come to me."
-Kabir

Most of us have prayed to God in our lives, often in distress and to receive material things: wealth or fame or recognition or good health or knowledge or love. Very few times, have we prayed to God out of total, unconditional love for him. If we seek God, we will attain God as well as wisdom and strength to handle worldly success - this is the essence of Shree Maa's message, "Love pure love". She often cautions people against focusing on name, fame and game, which ultimately can become their bondage.

SNEAKING OUT TO SEE SAINTS

Shree Maa:

Starting when I was eleven, I visited many saints, but my family didn't know because I would sneak out. Sometimes I went to a mountain or to a nearby Kali temple and I would sit down for many hours. Mostly I stayed inside myself. At that time my family thought I was stupid because I didn't say anything, but I had no attachment to them, just with my Grandma.

Some saints would cry, "Maa! Maa! Maa!" I went to see one sadhu and there were thousands of people waiting to see him. When I got there, he came out and blessed me. Lots of sadhus blessed me.

During Durga Puja at Navaratri (a special holiday honoring the Divine Mother), Durga was always with me, talking to me. (Durga, the Goddess who removes difficulties, is another form of Chandi).

Sometimes Durga would say that I needed to go to a particular place to see a sadhu and then she would disappear. This kind of thing happened lots of times. This was normal for me.

For example, King Himalaya's wife, Maina Devi, did tapasya (spiritual practices) in the mountains so that the Divine Mother would be born in her house. She wanted the Divine Mother to be her daughter. So Goddess Parvati said to Maina Devi, "I am coming to your house and I will be your daughter, but you will forget who I am when I am born. You will treat me like your daughter. This is my advice to you."

Maina Devi asked, "If you are coming to my house, why should I forget who you are?" Parvati answered, "Otherwise all human reality will go away. You have to treat me like I'm your daughter."

In this same way, sometimes God gave me darshan (vision) and then hypnotized me so that I wouldn't know what happened. A Goddess would appear right in front of me and I wouldn't feel anything. I knew that God created that moment. Similarly, Ramakrishna appeared many times.

UNCLE SADHU

When I was in sixth grade, one of my great uncles came to visit us. He was a great sadhu. He could tell your present, past and future by looking at your forehead. He was known for this all over India. He wouldn't say anything about me, but he wanted me with him all the time.

He wanted food only from my hand, but I didn't know how to cook. My Grandma supervised me and I cooked for him. When he ate, he said it completely fulfilled his desire for this life.

He took me here and there and told me stories about God and Thakur. He said that I have to do lots of work for this world, but I didn't pay any attention to that. I was completely detached. (Laughing) I didn't care what he said.

When he left, he wrote lots of letters to me saying, "Duty, duty, you have a duty." He went home and he always talked about me. I didn't realize then why he did that. (Laughing) Now I understand. After one year he died from a tumor that had turned cancerous. I was told he was thinking about me when he left his body.

He was the first person who opened my consciousness to who I am. Ramakrishna and Jesus were giving me instructions as I grew up. I didn't give it any mind (thought) because that's what I was familiar with. (Laughing) I grew up in a completely different world.

STUDENT DAYS

I was a normal student. I selected certain questions to study for my exams, but I never prepared more than that. I didn't give it much attention. For me, it was always Thakur, always Thakur.

Then I started to be a good student and all the teachers were surprised. I would look at a book and I would know it. I also led the prayer at the beginning of the day at our school for a couple hundred students.

I studied Sanskrit from sixth to tenth grade. When I was in tenth grade, there was only one Sanskrit teacher in town and he taught in twenty-four other schools. He was the most educated Sanskrit teacher in the whole area.

One day, with the final examination just three months away, while dictating some Sanskrit words to a girl in our class, he treated her badly. We had heard that he had done this before. I thought, "He is teaching God's language. How could his behavior be so bad? I can't tolerate this." I stood up and walked out of the class. I went to the headmistress and I said, "He is teaching God's language, why is he acting like this? I'm giving up my Sanskrit class." The teacher had used bad language.

The headmistress said, "You have only three more months before your final examination! You have been studying for three years. If you don't take the test you will fail."

But I insisted that I wouldn't go to class and when he came to class, I walked out. There was a course that one could take instead of Sanskrit called Hygiene. It included science, agriculture, human and animal physiology and it was also a three year class, eighth, ninth and tenth grades. But they wouldn't let me take this course instead of Sanskrit because it would be impossible to finish the entire three year course in only three months.

I kept this a secret from my family. So I asked Thakur, "What should I do now?" and he told me, "Go to the Hygiene class anyway and talk to the headmistress and it will be okay." So I went there and said, "Thakur told me to come and talk to you. Please allow me in the class. Give me a chance." So she did.

I studied for the Hygiene class day and night for three months. Then the exam that would measure the whole three years came and (laughing) I took it and got a good mark. It was so sad because I loved Sanskrit, but that's okay. So I graduated from that school and then I went to college.

In college I didn't want to study. I had become responsible for the care of my family and I was looking after the entire household. They wouldn't make any decisions without my advice. I was too busy to study and I had no time to open books.

Then a big storm came and Grandma went outside and fell down and damaged her lungs. From that point on, she was always sick.

One day I was meditating under the tree behind my house and I said to Thakur, (laughing), "Now what am I going to do? I don't want to study." Thakur said, "In your last life you didn't study and you felt sad about it. You have to study in this life." I immediately stood up and went to study.

Going to college was hard for me from the first day. I didn't want to open a book. Sometimes I would attend class, sometimes not. Finally exam time came and I was crying. I said to this big picture of Ramakrishna, "You told me to study. Why am I suffering like this?" (Laughing) I got really angry with Thakur and I turned his picture around and said, "I don't want to see you anymore!"

Thakur didn't give me an answer when I was talking to him that day. Generally, he always gave me answers. I went to the college, crying the whole way. When I reached the college, I found out that one of the questions on the test had been discovered by some students and they postponed the exam for three months. Isn't that something?

I came back home and hugged Thakur's picture and cried. I told him, "How kind you are. I didn't understand why you wouldn't talk to me." He was laughing and he said, "I don't want to talk to you all the time. Your heart is my heart. You have to understand me intuitively. Everything you do will be fine, have faith in yourself. I have been with you and you have never fallen. If I am your

Guru, then have faith and go forward." Nobody knew about these things that were happening with me and Thakur.

Shree Maa in college

SHREE MAA IN COLLEGE

(Laughing) I think that Ramakrishna arranged for that exam to be postponed. When I studied for the exam the next time, I had a feeling what the questions were going to be. When I took the final exam, I didn't know what was happening. My pen was just writing automatically. I passed my examinations and graduated from college.

It's very beautiful. It was Ramakrishna who tied me to my family. I was doing so much for them.

A BIG SNAKE AND MY FIRST SAMADHI

Once, when I was thirteen years old, I was staying with my second uncle during a vacation, and he had a big wooden Kali (Kali the Goddess who takes away darkness, is another form of Chandi) in his house. One day my uncle and aunt went to the dentist, and I was alone in the house. I was so happy because I could talk to Kali. (Laughing) So happy! I was folding clothes and I said to her, "Nobody is home. Could you come down and give me darshan? (Laughing) Please come down and give me darshan." I started crying loudly saying, "Please come down and give me darshan. Nobody is home!"

You wouldn't believe it but at that moment, I saw a big snake behind me at the window. I ran into the other room and closed the door and put towels in every hole. I was afraid the snake would come and bite me. It was an unbelievable snake, from that door to here long (over fifteen feet) and really fat and black with a hood this big (three feet wide).

I forgot that I talked to Kali and I was shaking and wondering what to do. After a couple of hours, I went out of the room to see if he was still there, but he was gone. Then I called some people who were walking on the road and said, "Come, you have to see, there's a big snake," but they couldn't find anything.

Then I got a fever and it felt like the snake was walking on my body. Ever since that day, I always know if there is a snake around. I can feel it. Sometimes I can sense a snake is around and I get a fever and feel like the snake is crawling up my arms. (Laughing) I completely forgot it all started when I was talking to Kali.

When I was sixteen and seventeen, I went beyond myself. I would automatically go into meditation. It's not like I would sit down and meditate, it would just happen to me. I was going into samadhi; I was becoming more and more subtle.

The first time I went into samadhi, it was like watching TV. I saw many different events that happened in my life. During this samadhi, I saw that big snake and Mother Kali said to me, "When you saw me you got afraid." Then I realized that the snake was Kali. Kali also told me that She was the light that was always by my side. After that first samadhi the light went away.

Then I forgot everything I saw during that samadhi until later, when I had devotees. Just like with Thakur Ramakrishna, there comes a time in your life to share these things with your children. I never thought it was important to share these stories before and I never told anybody about them, but Thakur said it was time to share them. Even Swamiji didn't know many of these stories.

Shree Maa in meditation

THE CRUNCHY MUNCHY SAINT

One winter day a big storm came and I felt something pulling me. I could feel that a saint had come. At that time my mom was living in the same town learning sewing and she suddenly came and said, "Do you want to see a sadhu?"

I had a habit of having a cup of chai at evening time with numkeen, an Indian crunchy-munchy snack. I went to drink the chai and found that we didn't have any more numkeen. That's the moment my mom came to take me. So we went through the storm and rain to see the sadhu.

We came to a house where many people were sitting and meditating in the living room. As soon as I entered, the sadhu opened his eyes and cried, "You came! You came! Sit down, sit down." He started to cry and said over and over, "You came, you came!"

I sat down in the back of the room near the door. Suddenly a big bag landed in my lap with a thud. (Laughing) It was numkeen! The sadhu knew!

After the meditation and arati was over it was ten o'clock. There were hundreds of people there, so I passed out the numkeen and then the sadhu said, "Come here and sit down. Sing, sing. I want to listen to your singing." He was very restless.

I sang Jago Tumi Jago and he was crying. I was surprised. He was shouting while I was singing, "Wake up! Wake up!" I was really impressed. He told me that I have to do lots of work for this world, reminding me again in the same way my great uncle had.

He invited me to come again and I would skip school to see him. I would pretend to go to school or I told the headmistress that my stomach was in pain. (Laughing) I did that a lot to see saints. When I saw him he was crying all the time. He said, "Lots of tests will come in your life."

After that I was completely different. I went a lot deeper, but I was not thinking about what I was doing, it was happening automatically. I was going into samadhi.

(Shree Maa pauses and looks intently) I want you to think about your lives as you read this book and your reactions to what I am saying. I have been talking about my childhood and how I grew up. Now you think about your childhood. Also write down the experiences you have while you are interviewing me.

When I talk about my life, then you think about yours. Then people will be more involved in the story. For instance, Agastya (an American devotee) told me he saw the Divine Mother when he was a child, but he forgot. You can dig into your own relationship with God. This is not only my story, I am telling the story of all human beings.

This is the first time I have ever told my whole story like this. I've told bits and pieces at times, but never the whole story in order. I feel Ramakrishna wants this story to be told now and you will be the historian.

Shree Maa by Richard Oddo

SHE IS THE ONE I HAVE BEEN LOOKING FOR

With Shree Maa's encouragement, I asked number of people who have known Shree Maa for a long time, to write their experiences. Here is Gabriela's story:

I was raised Catholic by my deeply religious parents. We attended services and mass every Sunday, went to confessions and took communions. I loved Jesus and His message, but didn't feel any connection to the rituals of the church. Over time I found myself "interacting" with God on my own without any formalities and intermediaries. My spiritual practice was extending to include meditation and yoga. Several years ago I went on a trip to a yoga convention. After spending the whole day doing asanas and exercises, we were getting ready to leave for the evening. Then I heard songs coming from one of the halls. "Cool! Live music! Let's go check it out!" I said.

I walked into a hall where a small frame woman wearing distinct yellow clothes was sitting very unassumingly on stage surrounded by band members. I did not know who she was or any one else in the crowd. But in that one instant, everything changed and my new existence began even though I did not fully realize the magnitude of the change at that time. When she sang, her voice was so sweet that all of us in the audience got up and danced. We couldn't help ourselves; the vibrations were too strong. Later on, a song list was passed around and we all joined her in singing. Several of the songs were Shree Maa's own. One composition in particular - written by Shree Maa when she was a little girl - stayed with me long after the evening ended. I found myself singing it over and over again.

Shree Maa spoke in Bengali and Swamiji translated in English. Although calling it a translation does not accurately reflect that evening's reality. Each word out of his mouth was so alive and true that it totally captured our attention - movement, time and space literally lost all meaning. I had very little knowledge of Hinduism, let alone about Shree Maa and Swamiji, but everything they said was spoken directly to me, for me.

After the singing was over, everyone lined up to receive a blessing. I also got up and stood in line, still mesmerized. Suddenly it was as though my chest exploded. I felt excruciating physical pain, which was followed by incredible bliss and serenity. Rivers of tears cascaded down my face and I sobbed uncontrollably. I felt embarrassed, happy and liberated all at the same time.

I went back to Chicago not knowing if I would ever see Shree Maa again. The evening seemed like a pleasant dream from which, unfortunately, I had to go back to my real life. Several months later I received a brochure in the mail outlining Shree Maa's and Swamiji's tour dates for the coming summer. "Nice," I thought, and filed it away. The next day, another copy of the same brochure came in the mail. "Ok," I thought. The following day and the next and the next I got more copies of the same brochure. Six in total! "Shree Maa! Very well, I will come and see you!"

I remember distinctly that their dates for Chicago was June 15th - 17th that year. I was scheduled to fly on an international route (I work for an airline) those exact days. I tried everything I could to get out of working at least on one of the three days, but nothing worked. I was totally frustrated and was speaking to myself, "Well, Shree Maa, if you want me to come see you, then please help me." The next day my work schedule was changed - just like that. I still don't how or by whom.

On June 15th, I made my way to the place where Shree Maa and Swamiji were going to be. Unfamiliar with the neighborhood and after getting lost and wandering for some time, I decided to ask someone for directions. I walked up to a lady and gentleman standing by a car. "Hi, do you know how to get to this street?" I asked. "Sure," she said. "Why don't I just take you there," and she dropped me off at the door. Wow! It should happen more often. I can get used to door to door drop-off services.

After the program I realized that I had no idea how to get back to the train. A gentleman (Fred as I learned his name later) was standing by the door and I decided to ask him for directions. "I am actually from Evanston (north of Chicago), but my wife Deb may know. Let me introduce you to her." Before I could say any thing, Deb had a friend drive me all the way home. Now I was really getting used to door to door transportation services.

Deb told me to be at her house the following morning very early if I wanted to see Shree Maa and Swamiji again. Next morning I walked into Deb and Fred's house and was startled with most unusual surroundings - no living room furniture, a makeshift altar and all kinds of people chanting, waving lights, waving incense and ringing bells. This is most certainly not what I would have thought of a church, but I immediately liked the concept of being the driver in this relationship with God instead of taking a cab. Shree Maa said that her mission is to make every heart and every home a temple and every one a priest. I was taught a beginner Siva puja. It was so simple and so powerful and that is the essence of Shree Maa. You are the priest. You invite the Divine to sit on your altar and receive your offerings.

I have spent time with Shree Maa on numerous occasions and the message is always the same: in simplicity and efficiency lies enormous power. This is not the power over others or over things outside, but instead the ultimate power within. She teaches this and more in every word and every action - more, of course, includes pure love or as she so beautifully says, pure devotion. Pure devotion is what pushes one to be simple and efficient never wasting time or resources for the loved one. This attitude of efficiency in turn makes a person one-pointed increasing the devotion exponentially.

For example, she decides to sew a skirt. I bring the material out and she folds it this way and that, cuts a pattern and almost instantly has a finished product. Had I blinked a second longer, I would have missed the whole thing. The same goes for her cooking; vegetables are chopped and put in the pan, spices added and the food is ready. It would have taken me longer just to begin thinking about what to make. She constantly reminds us the need for silently chanting mantra to keep us focused and to help control the constant chatter in our mind. She is always cooking for the Divine, God within all of us.

There is so much peace enveloping her, it's palpable. She inspires me to want to be just like her and she tells me how - with every word and every action with efficiency, simplicity and pure devotion. I have a long way to go and have to overcome many obstacles before becoming her or even like her. I know for sure that the journey has begun, my awareness has increased exponentially, the fight to control "I", the Ego, has become more intense. It is the first step, and, as a little child, I am faltering as I learn to walk towards her. I fall back to bad habits at times, but not without noticing it. I realize that the "I" is acting selfishly and I make an immediate correction.

My journey of transformation is a precious gift from her, bestowed upon me with pure love, without expecting any thing in return. I know that Shree Maa really does not need anything, but my heart wants to give her everything, do everything for her. I struggle to decide what precious gift I can give Shree Maa which is worthy of giving her. After a long struggle, I just give her my heart and pure love.

Shree Maa in deep contemplation

LEAVING HOME

Love once said to me, "I know a song,
Would you like to hear it?"
And laughter came from every brick in the street
And from every pore in the sky
After a night of prayer,
He changed my life when He sang
"Enjoy me."

Saint Teresa of Avila 16th century, Spanish saint

Evolved souls have often stated that it was very difficult for them to engage in mundane discussions or engage in domestic lives. Some even experience a painful sensation in their bodies when they have to engage in worldly affairs. These great souls long for solitude or to be with spiritually minded souls to share "pure love". Saint Teresa of Avila called God as Love and Shree Maa calls him as "Pure Love". In this interview, Shree Maa shares her experiences of meeting other great souls. It all started with her going into samadhi after her meeting the "Crunchy Munchy" saint and eventually led to her leaving home.

ONE WITH EVERYTHING

Shree Maa:

At the beginning of going into samadhi I couldn't keep any clothes on. If I kept them on, my body would feel like it was burning. I was going beyond myself and my family was getting nervous. I was gone most of the time (in samadhi).

They were worried that I wasn't eating. I told them that Thakur told me not to eat meat, but they yelled, "You have to eat!" One Sunday they forced me to eat chicken. I bit into the chicken and it felt like someone twisted my crown chakra and I fainted. After that, I completely gave up non-vegetarian food. I couldn't eat any meat or fish, just a little bit of dal and green vegetables. Eventually I couldn't eat that either. When you are in samadhi, when you go beyond yourself, the desire for food goes away, and you can't eat. I gave up everything and from that time on, I started losing weight. It was a big problem for the whole family.

At that time, I had lots of devotees and I would go to a Kali temple to hide. I entered a new level of consciousness in which I was one with everything, one with the whole creation. I saw no difference between me and anything else. I saw God everywhere. I would get on my knees and eat with the dogs because they were God too.

My family respected spirituality, but they never saw anyone go beyond with their own eyes. They had no personal experience of samadhi. They knew that some members of the family had been sadhus, who performed sadhana in the jungle, but they never saw it face to face in their own home. They thought I was crazy. Sometimes I would stay at the temple or someone's house and sometimes I would come home, but it was very difficult for me at home.

RAM NATH AGHORI BABA

A famous saint named Ram Nath Aghori Baba, who was 280 years old, came to the Kamakhya Temple. My mom told me, "We are going to see Ram Nath Aghori Baba, but you have to stay home. We don't want you involved with any more sadhus." Everyone went to see him and I stayed home and went into deep meditation. Suddenly I noticed a beautiful incense and datura flower smell. Everything was hugging me. I woke up and thought, "What's going on?" and I heard Ram Nath's voice say, "You have to come and see me." I said, "I don't have any money, how will I go?" and he said, "Go to the closet and inside the pocket of the white shirt you will find fifteen rupees." So I got up and went to the closet, and sure enough, in my uncle's shirt pocket I found the fifteen rupees.

I ran out of the house. I didn't care that the house was open, or that a thief might get in. When I went outside, a rickshaw was waiting there. Isn't that amazing? He took me to the bus station. A bus was waiting, even though it wasn't scheduled to be there. I took two buses and went to the Kamakhya Temple. When I arrived, Ram Nath Aghori Baba was just leaving. He saw me and he said, "You came!" and he blessed me and said, "Now you must take care of this world." Then he turned to the crowd of people bidding him goodbye and said, "This Shree Maa is an example of truth for the Kali Yuga."

A HUG FROM JESUS

One day I decided to leave home. I thought I would leave very quietly in the middle of the night and nobody would know. So at two o'clock, when everyone was sleeping, I started to leave. I tried to open the front door, but it wouldn't open. I looked up at a picture of Jesus that was above the door and He came down and hugged me. Then Jesus said to me, "Your time has not come to leave."

Then I fainted and when I fell down, the family woke up. "What happened? What happened?" they asked. They took me to bed and nobody ever knew about Jesus.

Later it was the right time to leave home. I went to each member of my family and told them I was leaving. They were crying and said, "What is going on with you?" I went to my eldest uncle and said, "I think it's time for me to go now." "You should stay here and study more," he replied. I said, "No, my time is now. I am going to Gauhati." For me going to Gauhati meant going to the Kamakhya temple, but my mom also lived in Gauhati. None of the family members supported my leaving except my Grandma, who gave me her blessing. It is strange that it was she who needed me the most.

A devotee got a train ticket for me and very early in the morning I left the house. Everyone was sleeping and I could feel they were suffering mentally. Even though I didn't ask for one, there was a rickshaw waiting outside that took me to my mom's house in Gauhati.

DEVOTEES GATHER

At Gauhati, people started gathering around me. Everywhere I went people wanted me to come to their homes. I would do puja with them and we would meditate together. Many sadhus called for me. They would be sitting in a temple or a hut and they would call me. Sometimes I would be sitting in the cremation grounds and wake up and see sadhus sitting in front of me.

During this time Subhash Chandra Bose (a great leader of the Indian independence movement) came to me in a dream and then a lot of his devotees came to me. Some Tibetan monks also came to see me and I traveled around with them. We went from village to village, teaching people how to live with dharma. We also taught them practical things that made their lives better. We made gardens, and taught them how to grow chilies and turmeric, and how to make chili powder and turmeric powder, which they could sell so they wouldn't have to beg.

I would go into samadhi at any time. I would be in the middle of doing something and then I would be gone. From morning to night I was in samadhi and then Shiva told me he would give me strength. He said that I would get something if I dug in the earth with a tool and I did that many times.

One full moon day, I was meditating and went into samadhi. Then I went behind the temple, where there was a jungle with lots of snakes and other creatures. When I saw them I fainted. I woke up and in my hand was a small trisula (a silver trident which is a symbol of Lord Shiva). I named it "Shankar".

And I still wear the silver trident around my neck.

MOTHER KAMAKHYA DARSHAN

From all over India, thousands of people would come to do sadhana at the Kamakhya temple and it became so crowded that there was no space to walk. During the three day period of Mother Kamakhya, I went with my devotees to the temple and I went into samadhi. My devotees were worried that I would leave my body. Once a day I would open my eyes for an hour and there would be many people around me.

When I am in Samadhi I don't experience any thing at that time. I don't know when I will go. Sometimes when I come back, I don't even know that I went somewhere. (Laughing) Somebody had to tell me.

When Mother Kamakhya's period was over, they opened the temple and thousands of people crowded toward the altar. Many people were being pushed aside. It was raining and I was standing in the line and when they opened the temple, a big, bright light came to me and I fainted. When I woke up I saw a bunch of sadhus were drying my cloth. Then Mother told me that now I could be free. I could go anywhere.

After that more people gathered around me. My mom got furious. Her ego was popping out. She thought, "What does she know? She is my little girl!" She became mean, very mean. She said bad things to me and to other people too. I think God was testing me, but I never changed. I thought to myself, "These people have too much ego." I said to God, "Show them who you are and who a divine being is."

Then I took an axe and hit myself many times in the head. My family thought I was trying to commit suicide, but I wasn't hurt in any way. When I hit my head with an axe and nothing happened, and then they believed. They thought, "My God, nothing happened to her! This is divinity." The forces of confusion surrendered. After that everyone bowed down to me, even my mom.

It's all lila (divine play). Sometimes we need to show divinity so the forces of confusion will see it. It's all part of the play. I didn't feel I was doing these things; it's just that they needed to be done.

Here we get a glimpse of metaphysical experience, which may be hard for a reader to relate with. However, many saints have documented similar experiences, including Sri Ramakrishna when he tried to cut his own head with a sword.

JUMPING

Then I left home and started walking. I walked and walked and by evening time I had reached the Brahmaputra River. I decided to end it all, so I jumped into the river. I felt it was time to go. I was with God all the time, but sometimes you want to see something. At a certain time this feeling comes, like when Ramakrishna took a sword and said to Kali, "Will you give me your darshan or not? If not, then I am going to kill myself." Then he was about to cut his neck with the sword and Mother Kali appeared in a big light and he fainted[2].

---

2 Please see story number two in the reference section.

You can't ask the question, "Why did he do that?" It's all a lila, God's drama of duality and non-duality. In this world you have to live with duality even when you are with God all the time. When you're in duality, sometimes God likes to cut that duality completely. God is doing it; it's His drama, His play. Otherwise, how can you jump off a riverbank? How could you be that brave? It's His lila and I had complete faith in God and I jumped. I tried to dissolve myself. I didn't know anything about this world. I can't explain this to you.

After I jumped, I saw a bright light and a big wind blew me back. Then a sound came from the sky and it said, "You can't leave. You have lots to do! I AM YOU!" I fainted and fell down on the stones and the light dissolved.

When I woke up, I was in a temple. A man had found me and took me to his Guru's ashram. It was a monastery of Aghori Baba, the 280 year old saint I talked about before. Isn't that connection interesting?

I didn't pay any attention to this unusual experience. I just went from here to there. I didn't know where I was going. Just went with no thoughts. It's beautiful. There are so many stories I wish I could tell you. One day a devotee, called Ambaba, prepared to cut off his own head. He said to Mother, "I am offering you my head, please give me darshan." And Mother appeared. Now who will believe this? What will people think if some one says this kind of thing? They will think the person is crazy.

I don't care (it is not the purpose) if they believe or they don't believe. The story of Ravana[3] is a true story. It's a real story, but who will believe that one man had ten heads! They won't believe it, because this is the Kali Yuga, the

---

3 Please see the reference section.

Age of Darkness[4]. You won't see divinity in the Dark Age. This is the fourth yuga and people need to understand that these kinds of things happened in earlier ages. If they knew the history of this world and how human beings came to be here, they would understand.

Again, the reader unfamiliar with mysticism is presented with an experience, which would appear to be a fairy tale or result of an over-active imagination. In my last twenty years of association with Shree Maa, I have witnessed many unusual experiences where I am left wondering if it was just a coincidence or something more than that.

LEAVING HOME FOR GOOD

Finally I ended up back in my mother's house and stayed there for a short while and then decided to leave for good. The day I was to leave, the house was empty because my mother had gone to work and my sister was at the market. When I walked outside a rickshaw was waiting and I told the driver to go to the train station. There was an important Ramakrishna temple on the way to the station and just as we went by the temple, the rickshaw tire punctured. I got out of the rickshaw, and although the temple was closed, the temple door swung open for me. There was a hibiscus flower on the altar in the temple and I took the flower and ate it.

I was in a totally different state of consciousness. I had no plan, but I knew that Thakur was taking care of everything. I got to the train station and suddenly a man appeared and said, "Mother, I have a train ticket for you to

---

4 Hindu cosmology identifies four ages, or yugas, in the history of this planet. The first age, Satya Yuga, was the purest and most spiritually advanced and the fourth age, Kali Yuga, has the most selfishness, hatred and delusion.

Bankura (the train station for Kamarpukur, Ramakrishna's birthplace).

Thakur had made arrangements for me. This seemed natural. I didn't know where he was taking me, but I had complete faith in Thakur. I completely surrendered to him.

Shree Ma after she left home

COMING HOME

You are sitting in a wagon
Being drawn by a horse whose reins you hold.
Most never hand the reins to Me
So they go from place to place the best they can,
though rarely happy.
And rarely does their whole body laugh,
feeling God's poke in the ribs.
If you feel tired, dear, my shoulder is soft,
I'd be glad to steer a while.
-Kabir, 16th century sufi poet

Christianity, Judaism, Buddhism, and Hinduism all have the same basic belief that life cycles do not start with birth and do not end with the death of a physical body. In fact, the life cycle has no beginning nor an end. As a part of, and in accordance with, the nature's law of renewing cycles, a soul sheds an old body and takes rebirth. There are differing explanations in different religions for a soul's rebirth. Buddhism and Hinduism believe that each reincarnation may be different, a soul may return as a lower or higher form of life depending on its karma. In western religious philosophy, a soul reincarnates to progress towards higher spiritual levels. Implied in this philosophy is the concept that a soul may reincarnate at the same level in case of no forward progress in a previous life time.

In this chapter Shree Maa reveals her previous birth as Sarada Devi, Ramakrishna's wife[5] and spiritual heir. Ramakrishna and Sarada Devi lived together as saints and as spiritual partners. Ramakrishna said that Sarada Devi was an incarnation of Saraswati, the Goddess of learning and wisdom. When Ramakrishna left his body after teaching his great disciples for only five short years, his ministry was left in the hands of Sarada Devi. She

---

5 See reference.

continued his teachings for thirty-four years, initiating thousands of disciples, and becoming one of India's most influential modern saints.

In our last talk Shree Maa had been given a train ticket by a total stranger to go to Kamarpukur, Ramakrishna's birthplace. The story picks up while she was riding on that train.

KAMARPUKUR

Shree Maa:

When I got on the train, I fell asleep and would have missed my stop, but the woman sitting next to me woke me up at Kamarpukur. I got off the train around mid-day. All I had with me was a small bag with a Chandi book and a few saris, that's all. I started to walk and eventually reached a pond called Haldapukur. I took a bath in the pond by going under the water three times saying the Gayatri mantra. When I got out, I saw a big snake right in front of me. It didn't feel unnatural and I had no fear. At that time, I saw everything as God. This state is called Sahaj Samadhi. I bowed down to the snake and he was very happy. Then I walked up the steps of the pond. When you are really divine, everybody is your friend; nobody is your enemy.

RAMAKRISHNA'S TEMPLE

A woman had witnessed my encounter with the snake and she said to me, "I was waiting for you." She was over sixty years old. She took me to the nearby Thakur temple. Suddenly, while I was sitting inside the temple, many stories came from my mouth. I started to talk about where Thakur was born, where he studied, the different sadhus that came to see him, the whole history of Thakur's life. I talked about how this building had changed since Thakur's time and how another building was here before.

Shree Maa told this woman intimate details of Ramakrishna's life that could only be known if she had lived during that time.

The lady took me to the president of the Ramakrishna Temple to see if I could stay there. The president said (Shree Maa impersonates the president using an imperious voice), "Without a letter of introduction, no one can stay here. I don't even know where you came from." I said, "Thakur sent me." (Laughing) It was so funny, he was looking at my shoes and he said, "You have beautiful shoes."

Then I sat down in Thakur's temple and I went beyond myself. I sat down at three in the afternoon and got up at eight-thirty at night. When I woke up, I saw lots of brahmacharis and swamis standing and watching me.

Then the president told me, "You have to eat prasad." I said, "I don't eat." The president was pushing me and said, "You have to take prasad." He took me to the dining room and gave me prasad. Several other women were eating there. I started to eat, and when they gave me cream of wheat pudding, a cat suddenly appeared and I fed it. Then I went into samadhi. When I woke up late at night, I saw that the women were irritated because I fed the cat.

The president was watching everything and he felt something inside. He was shocked because he realized who I was. He said to the women, "You don't know who she is. At the end of her life, when Sarada Devi ate pudding, a cat would always eat the pudding too. Mother (Sarada Devi) never ate pudding without offering some to the cat." After that the president really took care of me and told everybody else to take care of me.

That first night at Kamarpukur, which was Guru Purnima night (the annual celebration of the Guru), I didn't sleep. I opened my door around midnight and that woman (who had met me at the pond) was sitting in front of my door. She couldn't sleep either. She had a feeling that this person she had met was not a real human being.

So we walked around the whole village together that night. I started to tell her everything, "This is where Thakur studied; this was his school." Many stories about his childhood, about his life with his family, came from my mouth.

Knowing that the woman had many questions about Shree Maa's identity, including whether she is a real human being or not, Shree Maa decided to reveal the details of her previous life when she was with Ramakrishna as a means to remove anxiety and confusion in this woman's mind. I have witnessed Shree Maa's greatness many times, when out of her love and compassion for people, she would make herself totally accessible even to the point of abandoning her privacy.

Shree Maa:
She walked with me and cried and cried. The lady told me that when Sarada Devi got married, she used her family's ornaments for the wedding ceremony. Her family took care of Sarada when she was a child. Eventually morning came. We had walked the whole night; it was so great! That morning she went to her family and told them who I was.

 *Sarada Devi*    *Shree Maa*

JAYRAMBATI

Then I went to see the president of the ashram and said, "I am going to Jayrambati (Sarada Devi's birthplace)." The president said, "You don't want to stay here?" and I said, "I need to go to Jayrambati because Thakur is telling me to go." He told the woman I walked with to take care of me, so we went to Jayrambati together. Jayrambati wasn't far away, maybe forty minutes by bus.

When we got to Jayrambati, she took me to the president of Sarada Devi's temple. I don't know if the Kamarpukur president told him about me or not, but when he saw me, he gave me the room where Sarada Devi lived towards the end of her life. Generally they don't give anybody that room.

Every morning at three a.m., I chanted the Chandi. The president and many other people listened to my Chandi and cried. Sometimes I sang a song Sarada Devi used to sing and one swami always cried when I sang that song. One line went,

"Madhur Amar Mayer Hashi Make Amar Mane Pare, Mother is laughing, sweetly in my heart."

LIVING WITHOUT FOOD

This Swami loved me and every day he sent a boy saying, "Tell her to come to take prasad," but I refused. I had stopped eating completely since I had left home. When a pure devotee gave me some fruit or vegetable juice, I would drink it. Once in a while, when I broke samadhi, they would pour me orange juice or sugar cane juice. Sometimes they gave me green coconut juice. I drank lots of water. Every day they brought a clay jar of sandalwood water and I would drink that. I had sandal wood water and basil leaf water all the time.

When Swamiji came and requested me that I could not leave my body, I started taking blended fruit and milk. I also drank Horlicks (a malt beverage). Once in a while they gave me some boiled rice with ghee. It was hard to eat because my stomach had shrunk.

Everybody was surprised that I was living without food, and that's why people thought I would die. It didn't feel like I wasn't eating anything. I remember my whole body had a sandalwood smell.

I was different then. Now, when I compare my body to then, I wonder, "How did I survive?" and I'm surprised too. Now if I don't eat, (Shree Maa makes a funny voice as if she's in pain) "Oh, I'm hungry!" But one thing you must remember: When you are one hundred percent in another world with God, you don't need food.

SARADA DEVI'S FAMILY

One day I walked through the whole village telling stories about Sarada Devi and Ramakrishna. Sarada Devi's family started to wonder who I was. Another day I was sitting in Sarada Devi's temple in samadhi around five o'clock and when I woke up a man came to me, and said, "You came back! You came back! I was waiting for you! She told me you would come and you came!" He bowed down, sashtanga pranam (bowing while completely lying on the floor) and started crying. His name was Ganapati Mukherji and his aunt was Sarada Devi.

He took me to his home and he showed me articles that Sarada Devi used: her stone plates, worship utensils. He gave me Mother's asana (Sarada Devi's meditation seat). He was crying. I didn't pay attention to what he was saying because I was in a completely different world then, do you understand?

Every day when I went to do puja some energy was automatically taking me to the Kuladevata temple of Sarada's family. The Kuladevata is a family deity that has been worshipped for generations. I went to the temple and the door was closed. Then, as had happened before, the door automatically opened. I sat down and offered a hibiscus flower, and then I came back.

One of the priests was upset that I went to that temple and he asked others, "How did she get inside?"

I didn't care what he was saying. As time went on, the whole village knew about me and felt a connection to me. Some of them started to listen to my chanting at three a.m. Then Ganapati came to me and said, "I'd like to perform worship to you. Please come to my house."

So he took me to his house and he had me sit on Mother's asana and he performed puja to me. Well, I went into samadhi. It was about one o'clock and when I woke up around four o'clock there were many visitors watching me. When visiting Jayrambati, a visitor usually goes to the Sarada Devi temple, then her family's temple, and then they visit her family. So they had come to Ganapati's house as part of their pilgrimage.

One of the ladies visiting from Belur was a widow and she was very black. I said to her, "Oh, you came here, huh? Do you remember me? You tried to jump in the Ganges."

She really was shocked, you know, because nobody knew that she tried to commit suicide. When she was going to jump in the Ganges, she saw me. So when she saw me again that day, she was surprised. She started to cry. You can see how beautifully Thakur makes things happen.

After being at Jayrambati for two weeks, there was a big festival and lots of people were gathering. I locked my room because I knew Thakur was going to do something. I also felt that this would be my last day here.

Suddenly at midday, the president of the temple called me. He knocked on my door three or four times. Then he kept sending a little boy with a message. (Laughing) Finally, I had to open my door and go see him. I went to the president and there were maybe five hundred people there. The president said, "Come and sit with us and take prasad." You know, he didn't really force me to take prasad, but he pressured me. It was too much.

It was very interesting because the whole hall was filled except for the one place that I sat every day to take tea. I sat down and they brought me prasad. At that stage, when I was hiding myself all the time, it was scary to be with so many people.

I was just taking a little food, and suddenly a woman grabbed my hand and said, "You stop eating! Before you finish you have to tell me who you are!" I knew Thakur would do that. She continued, "Last night I saw you in a dream and that's why I came here today. You have to tell me who you are!"

(Laughing) I told her, "I don't know who I am. I came here because Thakur told me to come." I took my plate, got up and started walking. I knew something would happen; some disturbance would occur.

The readers might wonder why Shree Maa did not reveal herself to this lady when she had already told about herself to the woman at the pond. The answer lies in the mental make-up of the two women. The woman at the pond sat outside Shree Maa's room in the middle of the night, humbly wondering and waiting, while this lady publicly demanded an answer (her ego manifesting) by grabbing Shree Maa's hand and not listening to her inner voice.

Why should I tell her? She already knew; Thakur gave her darshan. Why am I going to tell her? What purpose would I have to tell her who I am? If I said who I am, then my ego would be coming out. I can tell her I am a child of God, that I'm an instrument of peace, but am I going to say (in a high pitched, funny voice), "Who am I? Sarada Devi." (Laughter) So I started to run away and she started running behind me and I was running fast.

I ran past the president, who was standing at the door giving betel leaves to a woman. I said to Ramakrishna inside, "Thakur, what are you doing today? If you really want me to tell her, give me a sign. If this woman comes to me and gives me betel leaves then I will know." So I ran to my room and closed the door. Then the lady knocked on my door and kept knocking, it was really incredible. Finally I opened the door and she gave me some betel leaves saying, "Mother, here, please accept these betel leaves."

Then I realized it was all Thakur's doing and I had to tell her now. I asked her to sit down and she asked, "You have to tell me who you are." I replied, "Who are you?" She said, "I am the magistrate's (chief of police's) wife. I feel you are Mother Sarada." I told her, "If you love Thakur, if you love Mother Sarada, and you have pure eyes, what ever you see is true." She cried and cried and finally said, "In my dream Thakur told me that you were Mother Sarada. That's why I came today."

Then she went back to all the visitors and told everybody! After that, a big crowd came and bowed down to me. People were crowding and bringing food. It started to disturb me. They were gathering outside my door. Also Sarada Devi's family invited me to go to this place and that. So the next day, at three o'clock in the morning, I left! Nobody knew, (laughing) the whole village was sleeping.

I walked for a long time in the dark. I had no idea where I was going. Eventually, Thakur took me to a bus station. There I waited for a bus to go to Calcutta. By God's grace, Thakur brought me a Calcutta bus and I reached Calcutta in the morning (traveling without a ticket). Thakur was taking care of everything! When you love God, He is protecting you, taking care of you all the time. I had God's work to do. God was completing his plan.

GOD IS ALWAYS WITH US

"I'm this, This is mine"
Idiot thoughts.
Oh Mind, you imagined all that stuff was real
and careless tangled the heart!
"Who am I? Who is mine?
Who else is real?"
Oh Mind, who serves and who is served?
All of this gladness and sadness are nothing.
Oh Mind, the light is snuffed by possessions,
Everything is lost in a dark room
So live in a wise house and be wary.
- Ramprasad Sen

For Shree Maa, God is both personal and universal. Her union with God is so profound and absolute that there is no longer a distinction between worshiper and worshiped. It is a spiritual as well as psychological conception. It is the true being, the true consciousness, the true delight of existence beyond the body, the mind, the life's vital force or heaven. She has crossed beyond all these planes in order to arrive at the higher plane of super-consciousness which is her foundation and home. From here, she guides us in our struggle between spiritual powers of light and darkness, truth and falsehood, knowledge and ignorance, death and immortality. Her key messages are through awareness of each moment with compassion and acceptance, witness thoughts coming and going, and feelings and sensations rising and falling. There is no individual self - just a passing show of thoughts, feelings and sensations. See every thing as God - meditate upon that being who is higher than the highest. He is the cause of eternal bliss. He alone resides within the space of Shree Maa's heart and illuminates her purest clarity.

In this conversation, Shree Maa explains the connections between the individual soul and the universal soul.

Shree Maa:

A divine soul always lives with everything and everyone in the universe. Divine soul means God, complete consciousness with the universe. When a devotee is very devoted to God like she was, a divine soul is always with them. When a divine soul meets a pure devotee, a divine soul will recognize them and know who they are and what their karma is. This is the relationship between a devotee and God. For example, you feel me sometimes. Why do you feel that? Because I am with you. Whoever has that connection, that devotion, he will feel that a divine soul is always with him, with oneness.

One time I was going to Rameshwaram by train with some devotees. In another compartment, two German priests were talking in their own German language. I was in samadhi and when I woke up, I told K.N. Parvat, "Go to that room, you'll find two Catholic priests talking about their ministries in India." He went and said, "My Mother said you were talking about your ministries in India. Is it true?

They said, "Yes, who told you?" They came to see me and said, "How did you know that? Do you speak German language?" I smiled. Then they knew I was divine and they were devotees of the divine too. They were trying to reach God, so there was a connection. They bowed down to me and invited me to Germany. A divine soul lives with each individual soul.

When the Jayrambati lady tried to jump into the Ganges, people stopped her. She saw the Divine Mother. She was calling for the Divine Mother, so I told her that I was there. She did not see me as a human being. She saw Kali, a form of the Divine Mother. When I saw her in Jayrambati and told her about the incident, she thought, "This is the Divine Mother."

When Ram Dass went to see Neem Karoli Baba, he read Ram Dass's mind. It's the same thing. Ram Dass was seeking something divine and he went to a divine being and the divine being knew who he was and what he was seeking. When you live in truth and do sadhana, nothing is hidden. Very few people can hide from me.

When maya is pulling you, taking away your mind, when you are swimming in maya, you can't think about God. At that time, you can't tell who a divine being is. Therefore you need to meditate and do sadhana. Then you will know you are not separate from any soul. Then you can recognize a divine being immediately. It is very beautiful and it is very easy, if we keep ourselves straight.

Shree Maa picks up her narrative after leaving Jayrambati and boarding the bus to Dakshineshwar.

So I got off the bus at Dakshineshwar (where Ramakrishna lived most of his adult life) and a man took me to the Krishna temple there. Do you know the

Ramakrishna story about this temple? One day the Krishna murti's (statue of Krishna) leg broke. Mathur Babu (a devotee who owned the temple) wanted to throw the murti away. Thakur said, "If your leg was broken, would you throw yourself away?" So Mathur had the leg mended.

I sat down at that Krishna temple and went into samadhi around seven o'clock. When I woke up, a very black woman was sitting near me eating betel leaves. She was dirty and red betel juice was drooling from her mouth. She had wild Kali hair. She said, "I knew you would come! Therefore I am here waiting for you. Mother, arati is over, it's after twelve o'clock, let's take some prasad." She gave me some of the Divine Mother prasad from the Kali temple and we ate together. After that, she took me to the twelve Shiva lingams on the Dakshineshwar grounds and she asked me over and over again, "Do you remember? Do you remember?"

Then she took me to Ramakrishna's meditation room. She said, "You go there and sit down." I sat down, and I was completely gone, and when I woke up, she was waiting outside. She said, "I rented a rickshaw. Now we will go to your place, Sarada Devi's place (the house where Sarada Devi lived near Dakshineshwar)." She told the rickshaw wallah, "Take care of her!" And the moment she said that, she disappeared.

When she disappeared, I wasn't surprised because this has happened many times in my life. I felt, "Thakur is doing his lila. Let him do whatever he likes to do with me."

When you are living in pure consciousness, you are living with the whole universe. Any form can come to you and you can go to any form. A pure soul is always connected with the whole universe. You are not different than anything in this universe. You are related to every atom in creation. When you reach that step, you can see so many things. You are completely different; you are dissolved.

When we arrived at Sarada Devi's house, it was closed. Suddenly, the door opened automatically. A monk came out and said, "It's closed now; you can't see anything." I told him, "OK," and I sat down outside on a bench and I went into samadhi. When I woke up, I saw a beautiful, young lady sitting with me. She asked me, "Hey Mother, where do you come from? Where are you going?" And I asked, "Who are you?" She told me her name and that she was studying English and she said, "I would like to be with you." I said, "I don't know why you want to be with me, but you can if you like." She asked me, "Where would you like to go?" I told her, "Belur Math (the main temple of the Ramakrishna Mission)" and she said, "I'll take you there." She took me to Belur Math up to the gate, and there she disappeared!

I went inside Belur Math and evening arati was done. I didn't know where I was going. I didn't know where I was staying. I didn't talk with anybody; I just walked. I walked through the Belur Math and started walking down the winding paths outside. It was a dark night and the road was small and narrow. Suddenly, I heard a woman shouting, "Mother! Mother!" I wondered, "Who is that calling me?"

It turned out it was the woman I saw at Jayrambati who had tried to commit suicide. Do you remember? She took me to her house and she prepared everything for me. Every second she was taking care me, she was very sweet.

She started telling the Belur town people the story of our meeting in Jayrambati and many people came to see me. A big gathering started. (Laughing) The whole Belur town was, what is the English, "Crazy for me."

One day I was sitting in that lady's house and Thakur said to me, "Now is the time to go to Orissa." So I said to the people there, "You know, Thakur told me to go to Orissa, but I don't know how to get there." It turned out that the women and all her family came from Orissa and her son worked at the railway department. He said, "Mother, don't worry, I will get a ticket for you and arrange everything."

I reached Puri and when I got off the train, a rickshaw wallah (rickshaw driver) came up to me and said, "Mother, where would you like to go?" I told him, "I don't know," because this time Thakur hadn't yet told me where to go in Orissa. I said, "Wherever you would like to take me, take me." The rickshaw wallah drove for a long time. Eventually, he took me near the ocean to an ashram called Bharat Seva Ashram. The rickshaw wallah told me, "Mother, sit down here and you can see the Swamiji. He will make arrangements for you," and he disappeared!

I sat down on a bench, and suddenly a tall man came over to me and asked, "Mother, where are you from?" There were several hundred people around that day. I told him, "I came from the Kamakhya Temple, and I need a place to stay." He said, "You sit here. I will make all the arrangements." He went to see the president of the ashram.

Soon the president came out to see me. He said, "I can't give you a place in the ashram, but I know the best place for you to stay!" The tall man took me to a house and they gave me a big, fancy room. It was the house of the main priest of the Puri temple and his name was Ramakrishna Mahavaktari. He said, "You stay here as long as you want." I wasn't talking at that time, just a little when I needed to. So I stayed there and I chanted the Chandi at three in the morning.

One night Thakur told me, "You have to go to the Temple now." It was a long walk on a dark night at two in the morning. There wasn't anybody around. (Laughing) Sometimes a jackal would yell in the night. I reached the Puri Temple and was just about to enter, when I saw a big, tall sadhu. He had ash all over his body and was completely naked.

In that moment I knew Thakur sent me to see this saint. He looked a little bit like Trailinga Swami. When he saw me, he started to shake. I stopped and bowed down to him and he bowed down to me. Then he closed his eyes.

I went inside the courtyard of the temple. I just walked a couple of feet and it felt like somebody was pulling me back. I turned around to walk back and I saw the naked sadhu. Then he disappeared in front of my eyes! Isn't that great? After that, I came back to my room and chanted the Chandi.

On the second day Ramakrishna Mahavaktari's son came and said, "Ramakrishna Mahavaktari wants to meet you. He is waiting in his room." I went to see him and he was really a divine priest. He looked at me and said, "Go to the next room; that is your place." I went to the next room and saw a big Durga statue and I went into samadhi. It was so beautiful. When I woke up, I came back to my room and sat, as always, in samadhi.

At evening time, I woke up and I saw the tall man was waiting to see me and there were many people with him. In fact, the whole village was whispering, "A Mother has come and she's so young!" The tall man was curious about me and a little doubtful. He was thinking, "This is incredible, I don't know if I believe her. I'm going to test her and see."

I didn't know he was going to give me a test! Lots of village people were standing there and the tall man said, "I'm really impressed with you! I know Ramakrishna is your guru. Did you perform sadhana like Ramakrishna did?" And I told him, "No! Whatever Ramakrishna says, I follow! Wherever he takes me, I go. He is doing everything, ask him!"

He became irritated, and yelled, "You're a liar! Now I need to tell you who I am!" He was the disciple of a very famous tantric guru, I forgot the guru's name, and he said, "I am his disciple! I can do anything I want to you! I will find out what sadhana you did!" I said, "Okay, you ask Thakur," and then I went into samadhi.

I don't know what the tall sadhu saw in me when I was in samadhi. When I woke up around midnight, a few people were still standing with him. He started to cry and he bowed down to me and said, "Give me your blessing. I grew up here, I'm getting old here, I did sadhana, I'm still doing sadhana, and this is the first time I have ever seen a real Mother. You are Parvati Devi, the Supreme Goddess!"

He started to tell everybody and soon the whole temple, and then the whole town was talking about me. The next day he came to me and said he would take me to a secret place in the Jaganatha Temple. He took me to many different secret temples. In the Jaganatha Temple they have a flag, and at a certain time on a certain day, they change the flag and he went to the top, and gave me that flag.

There is an arati at Puri that is very unusual. At arati time the Divine Mother gives someone the order to do arati. The arati is done with a big candle-holder that has 108 lights, which normally no one could hold. But when Mother gives the order to someone, that person can hold the arati light and perform arati. It's very interesting. If she does not give the order, then there is no arati. He wanted me to see that. On the following day, I told him I needed to go back to Calcutta. He got me a ticket, put me on the train, and told the ticket conductor, "Please take care of Mother, she's going to Calcutta."

TRAVELING TO SEE HER CHILDREN

When the Guest is being searched for,
it is the intensity of the longing
For the Guest that does all the work.
Look at me,
And you will see a slave of that intensity.
- Kabir

Though a man can easily accept knowledge as the widest power of consciousness whose function is to free and illuminate, yet he has difficulty grasping the real power that unlocks the most profound mystery of life. Some say in the heart or behind it, lies a mystic light, call it intuition, though not of the mind, yet it descends through the mind - a guiding force leading us towards Truth. So, the heart is nearer to the life mystery than the human intellect full of knowledge. In Shree Maa's heart completely liberated from desires, wrath, intense demands, greed and fallen life forces, dwells a spark of divine that is always connected with the Universal being and its manifestation of the

Universe. Shree Maa is always connected to us on many levels. Once in a while when we pause long enough, we touch upon the marvel of that connection.

Shree Maa explains her personal connections with her devotees in the following section.

Shree Maa begins:

When I initiate somebody, we are one soul. I can't leave them. They are with me all the time, when they're conscious (about the connection) they know it. When they're attached to other things, then those attachments are what they are aware of.

Do you understand? When you love somebody deeply, they are always with you? If you love God you become God.

This whole universe is my family. Sometimes a devotee has an experience that I physically visited them even though I was in another city at that time. They would say to me, "Mother, you appeared to me and we talked." Or they wrote me a letter and said, "Thank you for coming to me." People saw me in many different places.

When a devotee calls me, sometimes I need to go. I go in my subtle body. They will see me with their pure devotion. Some people will see me in their dreams, some will see me with their feelings - lots of devotees see me that way. That is natural, completely natural.

Once I was with them in Calcutta even though my physical body was in Gauhati. Even now I travel. One might wonder how it could happen. If you are completely with God, you can travel anywhere. You can do that. If you love God, you can do anything.

Krishna said, "I am everywhere." If you know Krishna, you can see me. When you really know God there is no difference between you and God. My actions are His actions.

WENDY AND SAM

The readers may be as intrigued as I was when I heard Shree Maa's statements above. In my research to understand the context, I came across Wendy's story, which she calls "Something magical is happening in my home and to my son". Here is Wendy:

My first encounter with Shree Maa and Swamiji was when my Gita study class was invited to visit the Devi Mandir. Before I left, I "signed on" to complete the Peace Sankalpa, and nothing has been the same since. The Peace Sankalpa is a commitment to chant a mantra from Chandi for world peace everywhere 100,000 times.

Once home, I started my recitations, sometimes silently and sometimes aloud. After a week or so, my 17 year old son started to imitate me - only he was saying sarva bgjklfda plkdj mdnkjm. In other words, he sounded out the first word and then just mumbled the rest. So I asked him if he wanted to learn the mantra, to which he responded enthusiastically - yes. He memorized it, and the English translation, in less than 5 minutes. He was quickly able to recite it quite fast and clear.

This might not seem that remarkable, however, my son is autistic. He is fairly high functioning, and has pretty good language skills, but I can assure you there is no way that I can get him to recite anything that he doesn't want to. I know, because I have tried! He now says the mantra every morning upon rising, and it is the last thing he says as he falls asleep at night. I have suggested for him to pay attention, and if he hears it in his head, to let it come through naturally. I also suggested that, if he is moved to do so, he can say it before his meals. If this continues to grow, I am going to get him a hand counter so he can keep track of how many times he says it each day. That is something I think he might like.

Last month, Swamiji blessed him with the gift of a rudraksha bead for healing, which he happily (and seriously) wears around his neck all the time. He never stops talking about Shree Maa. He listens to her sing, he wants to cook the recipes from her cookbook, sometimes he will sit next to me at the computer for the beginning of the Gita classes, and he keeps her picture in his room. Something magical is happening in my home, and to my son.

Last night, in Gita class, Swamiji answered my question about "those with small intelligence" and their ability to reach God. He said that those with limited mental capacity often have a pureness about them that allows them to see and know things more easily than the rest of us, due in part, to not having the same distractions the rest of us deal with every day. And yes, they can reach God.

My son is a very pure spirit, only seeing the good in others, assuming everyone loves him as much as he loves everyone, and now, he has connected to the loving energy of Shree Maa. He has actually said to me - "Maa can see my soul all the way from California. I know she loves me."

Shree Maa by Richard Oddo

SHIVA VISITS SWAMIJI

Shree Maa continues with the interview:

In the year 2000, we were in Benares and we were doing nine days of worship at the Annapurna temple there. We got there at two in the morning and once we got inside the temple doors were closed and locked until the temple opens for the public at 5 a.m. Swamiji was performing the Cosmic Puja and in the middle of his puja, he would go beyond himself. All of a sudden, at that particular point in Swamiji's puja, a man would appear and put ashes on his forehead and a garland around his neck. Even though Swamiji would reach that particular point at different times of the morning, this man would always arrived just at that moment, when he was saying the same mantra every day.

I felt so great! The first day he came, he stepped right on the Cosmic Puja, put his foot in the middle of all the flowers as Swamiji was laying them out! On that first day when he stepped on the Cosmic Puja, I was chanting the Chandi, and I looked at him and I thought, "This is Shiva!"

For nine days he came, and on the ninth day the temple was closed, nobody could come in. People were banging on the door, but they weren't allowed in, but while Swamiji was meditating, this Shiva Sadhu came to give a blessing. On the ninth day he disappeared and we never saw him again.

God comes many times in many different forms. I think it is our duty as human beings to look inside everybody - instead of looking at their five-element body, look inside at Shiva, and bow down quietly. If you do that, you won't get as caught up in maya. Inside this five-element body is something eternal. Try to relate to that in everyone all the time. This is a tool to reach God. We do our duty and inside we bow down to the eternal in others. Then enjoy whatever Shiva likes to do.

(Laughing) It's so beautiful! But it is hard for people to remember Shiva these days and it's even harder to see Shiva inside other people. When people are bound with the desires, anger, greed, and lust, and these are pulling people down, divinity is completely lost.

There is a story about the guru Goraknath[6]. There is another story about Trailinga Swami[7]. In this way, pure energy always expresses itself, (laughing) but nowadays, it's very hard to find. It's because of karma, lifetimes of karma.

ANSWERING THE CALL

Oh friend, if you are in love,
Then why are you asleep?
If you have found him, give yourself to him,
Take him.
Why do you lose track of him,
Again and again
If you are about to fall
Into heavy sleep anyway,
Why waste time
Smoothing the bed
And arranging the
Pillows.
-Kabir

We all have experienced a state where one feels emotion so powerful that tears come to one's eyes - not of sadness or happiness, it does not correspond to any particular feeling that can be articulated, but it is an

---

6 Refer to section 6 of the reference section for story of Goraknath

7 Refer to section 7 of the reference section for story of Trailinga Swami

intensity of emotion that comes from something that is clearly, precisely deep within. These emotional vibrations when contained, condensed, concentrated can achieve extraordinary things. All kinds of miracles can be done out of this "pure love" which is selfless, which demands nothing in return, which expects nothing in return. Shree Maa's love by the purity of its own nature and the divine instinct within it, feels and knows spontaneously in a much more direct and luminous way than the highest possible intellect, which suffers from limitations of physical perceptions.

In this talk, Shree Maa picks up the narrative of the story which exemplifies her selfless love to all beings without exception.

CALCUTTA SATSANGHA

Shree Maa:

I went back to the Belur lady's house. During that time, lots of devotees started to come to see me. A man came every day, he had a big tumor inside his ear and he was very worried about having an operation. I gave him a blessing, and his tumor broke. He became a great devotee and. I stayed for a long time at his house.

Then I started to go here and there. Lots of devotees were calling me. It became a big thing. Now I'm thinking, "Big thing," (laughing) at that time I didn't have those kinds of thoughts.

In 1976, I stayed at Gopal Chakraborty's house in Calcutta. Every evening people would come and after my samadhi broke, many words would come from my mouth. Discourses would come and I would give people advice about their lives. Everybody listened in silence. When I was in samadhi, it was almost as if everyone else was in samadhi too. Several hundred people were there and then many people from Calcutta started to come. When it got too crowded I left, that's the way I was.

Devotees gather for Shree Maa's Satsangha

After that, I didn't tell anybody when I was in town. You know, if there was some purpose for me to come, I would fulfill that purpose.

In 1976, I was mostly in samadhi from morning to night. I told Gopal Chakraborty, "Give me some ruled paper so when something comes to me I can write it down." Thakur told me many things, which I did write down. There were many pages and Thakur told me how to organize them. Thakur told me, "Within six months, Belur Math will host a big convention, like Vivekananda's world convention." I told Gopal's wife, because they are very devoted to the Belur Math, "Go to the president and tell him to organize this convention." They laughed.

The president said, "I don't think that after Vivekananda anybody in the Ramakrishna Order can do such a convention again." They didn't believe it would happen, but it did happen within six months. I was in Gauhati at that time, so I came back to Belur Math. I brought some of the writings that Ramakrishna dictated to me and told Gopal to read them at the convention. The president told them that day, "Please hide her. Don't take her out and make her a public figure."

I started to travel all over India with my devotees, performing pujas and meditation. Also, I was caught by the Bengal government. If they wanted to establish a foundation or hospital or school, they took me there for blessings. So all these demands started to come from the children, constantly pulling me here and there.

AN ENLIGHTENED SADHU CALLS

I kept going back to the Kamakhya Temple. Once a year Mother Kamakhya's period is celebrated at the temple and for those three days I was behind closed doors and was only drinking one glass of water a day. The Mother Temple was closed, and I was closed - off duty. Suddenly, after three days, I got an inner call to go to the Kamakhya Temple. I went there, and there was the saint who had called me. He was a very big naga man, a naked sadhu. He was a giant! When he saw me, he started to cry, "Bhagavati came! Bhagavati came!" He cried and cried; he was very happy. After that he and I both went into deep meditation for many hours. We never said a word.

After I saw that saint, I left. I have a deep connection with him all the time. Still now I have a deep connection with him. He's not on this earth anymore, he left his body, but still I have a deep connection with him and with so many other sadhus.

I could see that this sadhu was enlightened. Many sadhus came to the Kamakhya Temple, but he was really calling for Mother and his devotion pulled me. When a real sadhu, a pure sadhu, sees another pure sadhu, there is no talking. When a soul realizes who they are, there is no separate soul; there is only one soul. When we love God with a pure heart, there is no difference between us and God. We are one. I am everywhere.

When Ramakrishna went to see Trailinga Swami, Trailinga Swami wasn't talking at that time, so Trailinga Swami made a gesture to Ramakrishna of two fingers. Ramakrishna made a gesture of one finger to Trailinga Swami. That's all you have to say.

A KALI SADHU

At that time I would walk, walk and walk. Where I was going I didn't know. Ultimately, after three or four days, I found myself at the top of a mountain. A saint was doing sadhana there and he was calling me! He was bringing me there. There was nobody else at the top of the mountain, just wild jungle. I didn't have any food, I didn't have anything. I was alone but I didn't care. (Laughing) I didn't even know I was alone! I just knew that God was holding me.

This saint was doing Tantric Vidya sadhana to Chinnamasta Kali. There were five or six dogs there. I remember one dog was barking at me, but he didn't do anything. I went inside the temple - a beautiful temple with a big howan kund (ceremonial fire pit). I sat down and the sadhu saw me, and he said the same thing, "You came! You came! I was waiting for you!" He did puja to me, but he could not feed me because I went into samadhi. When I broke my samadhi in the evening, he was calling, "Maa, Maa, Maa!" Then I got up and left and never looked back.

If anybody called me back, I never looked back. I never got attached.

At that time I always had lots of devotees around. Sometimes I was alone; sometimes I would get up at midnight or at two o'clock and walk away! Sometimes I would leave from a devotee's house, because they would try to make me attached. They would say, "Don't go, don't go!" but I left anyway. I was strong in this way. That was the way my life was going.

Swamiji says it was inconceivable at that time for a woman to travel around India alone. It was even more inconceivable for a woman to travel alone into the jungles of the interior of Assam, without money, possessions or care. "What risk, what fear? When I am one with the soul of existence, how will anyone or anything cause me harm?" Therefore I was always in trouble with my family.

SURPRISE VISIT TO CALCUTTA

I can tell you another story. I was sitting in my room in Gauhati, and suddenly I received a message (intuitive) from one of my Calcutta devotees, K.N. Parvat was calling me because he was leaving his family to become a sadhu. He was an officer in the West Bengal Education Department. The next day I went to Calcutta, and stayed at a devotee's house. I said to that devotee, "Lock your house for three days, nobody should know I am here. I have important work to do." For three days they locked the door with a big lock because people sometimes get an intuition that I am in town.

Somehow Vashishta got the scent that Mother had arrived and he came and brought milk from his cow one night. When he came, he saw the big lock, and he said, "Hi, Mother!" He was so upset, you know. He had a feeling that

Mother had come and it was a true feeling! How beautiful is a soul's devotion! So he left the milk there and he went home, what a beautiful relationship!

When you really love me with a pure heart, you will always get the message. If you really love me, you would not do anything without me. We are one soul. Then you will know right away. That's purity. Pure consciousness is one; it is not separate. There is always a connection.

At that same time another devotee, Joydeep, was also getting a scent that I was here because he loves me so much. He came and saw the locked door also. He went back to his house, thinking, "I don't know, I'm feeling Mother is here."

Ultimately, I sent for Joydeep and told him, "I need to go to K. N. Parvat's house at two o'clock in the morning. You have to take me." He was so happy! He thought, "I knew Mother was here!"

So we went to K.N. Parvat's house in south Calcutta. His wife stayed in one room with the children, and he slept in the other room where he had his altar. When his wife opened the door, I put my hand to my lips saying to her, "Don't make any sound." I went through the door to his room. At that moment, he was wearing a little gamsha (towel), and he was bowing down to the altar. When he looked up, I was standing there. You can imagine that moment! (Laughing) Who would come at two o'clock in the morning? From Assam? He cried and cried.

That night, he was planning to leave his family; he wasn't going to live there anymore. He was going to the jungle, to the Himalayas, to do sadhana. He was only going to take a blanket and the gamsha he was wearing. He couldn't believe that I came, and that I caught him. I told him, "You can't leave your family. You have a duty to fulfill."

I took him to Dakshineshwar that day and said, "Go in the Ganges and say the Gayatri mantra." (Laughing) After that do Kali puja and then go back home. Your time hasn't come." He did what I suggested, and he became a great devotee.

THE GARLAND

The next day, Joydeep, who was a school principal, said to his wife Parvati, "Let's go see Mother again tonight." And his wife said, "I'm not going! I don't believe in her, you go." He got mad and said, "Today you will believe in her!" She said, "If she gives me a garland today, I will believe that she is a true sadhu."

So that night she came. I was in samadhi and when I'm in samadhi people put many garlands on me. When I opened my eyes, I took a garland and put it on Joydeep's wife and she started to cry, "Forgive me! Forgive me!"

It was like Girish Ghosh and Ramakrishna! (Laughing) When Girish Ghosh wanted to know who Ramakrishna was, Ramakrishna gave him proof. Some times, children want that kind of proof.

IT IS YOU

For most of us, it is extremely hard to fathom these stories but we believe Shree Maa because our own experience of being with her is extraordinary and profound. Just look into her eyes and see something unfathomable. I still wonder, "Who is this person?" My answer is that she isn't really a person, but something different, something not of this world. Paul Buchanan shares his first encounter with Shree Maa in his own words:

I'm always astonished by the rhythm that vibrates and courses through this world. I've always taken great solace in nature, letting the song wash over me. However, when I came face to face with a human manifestation of that harmony at the Devi Mandir, she shook me to my core.

A few years ago, I was pursuing a relationship with a most wonderful woman who, unbeknownst to me, was Shree Maa's disciple. During the first several months of my relationship with Seema, I couldn't help but wonder why she was always busy during the weekends. When prodded, she would vaguely allude to her family in Napa that she visits on the weekends. I knew that Seema is a very private person and I had yet to earn her trust. Eventually, I did earn her trust (and most importantly for me, her love) and this mysterious place in Napa began to take shape. I heard about Swamiji "Swami-who?"; (OK, I was raised Catholic), the Devi Mandir, her many friends and most often about Shree Maa. She always told me they were her family. It took a while before I realized these were not her blood relatives. She told me that about a month before we met, she and Shree Maa were walking at the Devi Mandir and Shree Maa suddenly said, "There is a Paul I have not met yet." When I heard this, I declared with full confidence, "Well she obviously means me and you have to take me there." I was just beside myself with curiosity and couldn't wait for Seema to take me to this place. Seema and I were sure by now that we would spend the rest of our lives together as husband and wife.

California is my home and I've lived here my entire life. The beautiful California out doors - the Coast Ranges, Sierra, Redwoods and wine country are my favorite stomping grounds. So, when Seema and I went on a May evening for the Saturday Program to Devi Mandir, I did not know what to expect. As soon as we stepped out of the car,

I was struck by the Devi Mandir atmosphere - most beautiful and peaceful. It was dusk and as we were making our way up the road Seema says, "Here comes Swamiji!" Coming down the road was an American man dressed in orange with a big, bushy beard and the most curious eyes (trust me, those eyes don't miss much. There is such a light there, an intense awareness). Seema had already prepped me on how to greet people with a Namaste, but Swamiji wanted me at ease and just stuck his hand out and said "Hello, nice to meet you" with a warm smile.

After parting ways with Swamiji, Seema and I continued to the temple (a modest building at this time, not the beautiful place of worship that is there now). As I was removing my shoes to enter, Seema told me that Shree Maa was coming. I'd like to stop here and tell the readers something. I did not want to write this article. I can still recall that evening vividly, the evening that shook me to my core. Conveying this story in words seems akin to trivializing it. Meeting Shree Maa for the first time is most unsettling. If one hasn't met her, trust me, one has not met the likes of her before. Sharing this experience can only lessen the reality. I do so because it is important for all of us to know that a human can evolve to this height of greatness.

I looked down the path, and because it was dusk, it was difficult to see. There was a group of people and in their midst was a slender figure that, as I told Seema afterwards, looked as though she was floating up the path. A silent voice carried up the road saying, "Don't be afraid. You're in a different world now." Swamiji standing next to me, raised his arms and said loudly "Welcome to the New World." Not sure of what just happened; I just stood there rooted to my spot while the group, Swamiji and Shree Maa entered the building.

It was apparent that Seema having a boyfriend was pretty big news and people were curious about me. I met many people who were very nice and seemed genuinely happy. There were also some that appeared wounded and struggling. Seema told me later, this is an Ashram and here any one can find a shelter. Soon after I settled in, I realized my big mistake - wearing a jean and not bringing a pad to sit on. I was immensely uncomfortable as the program progressed. Just how long can these people sit in one position? My legs were falling asleep, my butt was hurting, I couldn't understand 99% percent of what was being said. Clearly, I did not belong here. But I couldn't keep my eyes off of Shree Maa.

I remember the group singing a devotional song. At one point it became apparent no one was following along the lines or melody or the tune properly and the song was breaking down badly. Suddenly Shree Maa called out "Come on, what's going on here!" The group found their lines pretty quickly! So, this is a woman who takes singing seriously.

After the program ended (what seemed an eternity), every one began to line up in front of Swamiji and Shree Maa. I asked Seema what was going on. Seema told me that the people are lining up to receive a blessing. I very diplomatically stated that I should wait here but Seema told me in an equally diplomatic manner that it would be good to get a blessing. So I hesitatingly joined the back of the line. I was a bit alarmed (an understatement to say the least) to see that some of the people in front of me were lying prostrate in front of Swamiji and Shree Maa while others were bowing down touching their heads to the floor. Was this expected of me? As I debated in my mind how I should act, I suddenly feel Shree Maa regarding me. I was uncomfortable before, now I am down right nervous. It is my turn and I take a knee in front of Swami thinking it is a safe, respectful position. Swamiji smiles and offers me what appears to be yogurt and I extend my left hand to receive it. He gently asks me to offer my right hand to accept the prasad. Seema really could have prepped me better. After tasting the yogurt I slide over to Shree Maa and I am now face to face with her when the full impact of her being envelops me. I feel completely exposed. She casually asks me, "Have we met before?" and I blurt out in partial daze, "Yes, I think so." "Would you like a blessing?" and she places some ash on my forehead. As I walk away feeling unnerved and unsteady, a petite woman approaches me and hands me a book (Before Becoming This) and says Shree Maa wants me to have this. I feel a genuine bliss deep down in my heart to have received a gift from her.

Much to my delight, food is being served now. As I was enjoying a plate of delicious food held in one hand and a cup of rice pudding held in the other, I notice Maa is walking towards me - again with the same effortless movement. I say to myself, "Is it my state of mind or does this woman seems to just glide along." As she nears me, a thought occurs, what if she is going to shake my hand and my both hands are occupied with food. As though Shree Maa reads my dilemma, she tells me, "Hand me the cup" and then takes my free hand. Now I am completely and utterly immersed in her, I notice nothing but her. I remember nothing of what she says to me and it's only afterwards that Seema tells me what she said; "You need to get to know us better and we need to get to know you better." She then smiled and walked away.

On our drive home all I could think about was Shree Maa. My mind was totally at peace but completely energized. Never had I met anyone like her. The force of her uplifting energy is like nothing I've experienced before.

I was completely in awe, in love. Her beauty took my breath away.

There really is divinity within human beings and I had just experienced it first hand. Divinity in Shree Maa comes from being a very simple person; she is not complex, she has no guile, and there are no hidden agendas. What Shree Maa embodies is love, an unconditional pure love. But what is this unconditional pure love? I realize it's the tune, the harmony that pulses through everything in the universe. Shree Maa is so much in tune that she is transported by it.

Fast forward a few years, Seema and I are married and now living in a house in Sacramento. One lazy afternoon we were lounging around the house and the conversation turned to Shree Maa. We had been to the Devi Mandir the previous evening and Shree Maa had sung a song, which was so powerful it made me cry (even though I did not completely understand the lyrics). As Seema and I are talking about her and the previous evening, the phone rings. Seema answers the phone and it is Shree Maa. Seema hands me the phone and says, "Shree Maa wants to talk to you." Suddenly, I'm like a little kid and excitedly say "Hello Maa!!" She says hello and asks if I have time for a short story. "Of course Maa," I reply and she proceeds to tell me the following story (as I remember it):

There was a Guru who was always naked, never wore any clothes. He had many devotees. One day a devotee went to the Guru's home and knocked on the door. "Who is it?" asked the Guru. "It is I," answered the devotee. And the Guru did not open the door. The devotee was upset and left. The second day the devotee went back and again knocked on the door. "Who is it?" asked the Guru. "It is I," responded the devotee again. The Guru did not open the door. The devotee was again saddened and went away. The determined devotee went back on the third day and pounded on the door. "Who is it?" asked the Guru. "It is I," cried out the devotee in anguish, and the Guru went silent and did not open the door. The fourth day the devotee went back to his Guru's home and gently knocked on the door. "Who is it?" asked the Guru. "It is you," replied the devotee in silence. This time the Guru opened his door.

After Shree Maa finished the story, she asked me if I understood the story. Although not sure if I comprehended its meaning - is it living in complete silence or completely surrendering to Guru or both, I told her yes. Shree Maa laughed and said goodbye. After I hung up the phone, Seema asked what Shree Maa had said and I repeated the story Shree Maa had just told me. When I finished, Seema's face reflected the astonishment I felt. You see, when I'm around the house and not expecting guests I'm usually without clothes.

This bodily appearance is not all;
The form deceiving the person is a mask;
Hid deep in man celestial powers can dwell.
His fragile ship converses through the sea of years
An incognito of the imperishable.
A spirit that is a flame of God abides,
A fiery portion of wonderful,
Artist of his on beauty and delight,
Immortal in our mortal poverty.
This sculptor of the forms of infinite,
This creed unrecognized Inhabitant,
Initiate of his own veiled mysteries,
Hides in a small dumb seed of his cosmic thought.
- Sri Aurobindo, 19th Century Philosopher

FAITH AND DOUBT

Are you looking for me?
I am in the next seat.
My shoulder is against yours.
If you really look for me,
You will see me instantly
You will find me in the tiniest house of time.
Students ask me, what is God?
He is the breath inside the breath.
-Kabir

Shree Maa began this interview by describing another episode in her life, which, like others, is rooted deeply in mysticism and faith.

Shree Maa:
One night, at three o'clock, Ganesh appeared to me and said, "Tomorrow morning you have to go to the Brahmaputra River and protect a big ship."

At eleven a.m., I said to all the devotees who were with me, "Hey, does anyone want to come with me? Let's go to the Brahmaputra River. Today we'll have fun!" Everyone came with me - about a dozen devotees. When we reached the Brahmaputra River the port authorities announced, "Today no boat or ship is going to cross to the other side because of a big storm." At that time I knew, "Oh, this is why Ganesh told me to come!"

The devotees wanted to go back, but I said, "I'm sorry. I'm not moving. I'm sitting here. I have to find out why Ganesh told me to come." After about two hours, there was an announcement that a big ship was arriving, and that it would load quickly and depart. When the ship landed, I stepped on it and so did all my devotees, as well as many other people.

Oh my God! When we were in the middle of the river a big, big storm came! Later we learned that it was the biggest storm in fifty-three years. The waves were so big! The ship was going back and forth, up and down. It looked like the ship was going to go underwater. Everyone was being tossed about, the way God tosses us about sometimes. The ship's captain and others were crying, "Call on God, only God can save us!" and all the people started to cry!

I was so happy, you know, because Ganesh told me what he did, and I went into samadhi. Whatever happens - happens. Ganesh told me He will protect us. I heard later that the engine broke. The ship's captain, who was from England, was reading the Bible and trying to calm the crying people.

After a long time, I suddenly felt everybody holding me. I woke up and all the devotees were yelling, "Why did you bring us here?" All the children were shaking me! They were really upset and they were crying. They pleaded, "Save us, save us!" I said, "Just be at peace. Remember God," but they continued to cry.

I said in my mind to Ganesh, "Do you want to kill them? I know you want to protect them." I opened my eyes and asked the devotees to pray to Ganesh.

Then evening came, and slowly, with God's grace, the ship went near the Kamakhya Temple and stopped. It was supposed to go in the other direction, but it went instead to the Kamakhya Temple. Can you believe that? The captain pulled up, and many boats came, and everyone got down. Then the storm stopped!

People felt that I had saved them and they bowed down to me. They were so thankful. Then I told them to go to the nearby Shiva temple. All of us were praying to Shiva about what had happened that day! Everybody became very relaxed and happy. (Laughing) There was such a beautiful feeling that God is living with us, and God is protecting us all the time.

I had no idea there would be a storm. I had no other information; Ganesh said, "You go to Brahmaputra River today and take care of the people." It impressed me how beautiful it is when one loves God.

Do you know the story about a disciple who was asking his Guru how he could see God? The Guru said, "Let's go for a swim." The Guru took him swimming and held his head underwater until he could barely breathe! When he finally let the disciple up for air, as he was gasping for breath. The Guru said, "When you want God as much as you wanted to breathe just now, you will find him."

When you reach the stage when you really want God, this is how you feel! It feels beautiful. In this story, the disciple wanted to know how it feels and the guru put him under the water to show him. When the disciple was struggling to get back his breath, it was like when you are under the spell of maya. When you are bound with maya, you can't breathe.

So when the guru pulled the disciple to the surface, he let out his breath and said, "Aaah!" "Aaah!" That "Aaah" is exciting. You get a release when the guru lets you up. You feel what you really want, Maya or God? (Laughing) This was happening with all my disciples that day to remind them of God. After that, they all went to the temple and prayed, "Oh, God!"

It was so great! So great! A couple of devotees came with me, like Gautam and his wife. Gautam's wife had a little doubt, you know, "Oh, why is my husband going with this lady?" But after that she completely changed! She bowed down to me and said, "Mother, forgive me. I had a doubt about you." God gives a teaching in so many different ways; it's unbelievable.

DOUBT

I don't think a pure soul has doubt. When you love God, there is no doubt. When there is confusion, when you don't know yourself, then doubt surrounds you. Whoever lives with Maya, they have doubt. They are attached to their own desires. They have doubt, but doubt can help sometimes. Out of doubt, faith comes. St. Francis said that. Where there is doubt, give us faith. Without doubt, how will faith come?

Pure knowledge, pure wisdom and pure love are great weapons that can destroy all doubt. Here's a good story. Three sadhus were doing tapasya. Suddenly, the great sage Narada Muni appeared. The three sadhus saw Narada Muni, and said, "How long will it take us to see God?" Narada replied to the first sadhu, "It will take you 100,000 years!" The first sadhu was very unhappy. Narada told the second sadhu, "It will take you 200,000 years." The second sadhu was extremely unhappy. Finally Narada turned to the third sadhu and said, "Do you see this tamarind tree? This tree has millions and millions of tiny leaves. That's how long it will take you to see God." The third sadhu was overwhelmed with joy! "That means I will see God!" He danced around and around in joy and in that moment he realized God.

EVEN GREAT SADHUS HAVE DOUBT

There was a moment when Ramakrishna was dying and Vivekananda (then known as Naren) was in the room with him. Ramakrishna appeared to be preoccupied with pain. Vivekananda thought, "Could this suffering man be an incarnation of God? If he would declare his divinity now in the face of death, then I'd accept it." A few moments later

Ramakrishna turned to him and said, " Oh Naren, aren't you convinced yet? He who once was born as Ram, and again as Krishna, is now living as Ramakrishna within this body." So is doubt so powerful that even Vivekananda, Ramakrishna's greatest disciple, had this doubt while Ramakrishna was dying?"

Even Arjuna had doubts with Krishna. Krishna showed Arjuna his Vishvarupa, his divine form, at Kurukshetra. Krishna showed who He was, "I am everything. Look at Me; the whole universe is who 'I am.'" After that, Arjuna thought, "OK, now I know who you are, now I am ready to fight." But when the fighting started, Arjuna sometimes forgot. At times he didn't even obey Krishna's orders. When Krishna told Arjuna, "OK, now it's your time to kill Bhisma," he couldn't do it. Krishna had to show His form several times again. After that, Arjuna became strong, and he did kill Bhisma. When the fighting started, Maya, illusion, sometimes covered divinity, because Maya is very strong. When Arjuna became lost in doubt, Krishna was there reminding him of the dharma.

Maya always covers; I can't tell you it never happens. It will happen as long as we are alive in this world. Talking about Swami Vivekananda, he did have doubt. He said to himself when he first met Ramakrishna, "This man is very powerful, is he tricking me?" He needed to clarify this for himself and he did! It was the same way with Arjuna and Krishna. When Krishna showed Arjuna his  divinity, He didn't show His divinity one time. He did it again and again to remind him. How much patience, how much love he had! Always that relationship between God and man is going on, cutting the ego.

Vivekananda didn't do sadhana until he was seventeen years old. He was a student of Vedanta. After Ramakrishna left the body, he started doing sadhana. He knew his responsibility then.

If you keep your tapasya, there comes a point when doubt is erased. But if you can't keep your tapasya, everything will topple (even after attaining enlightenment).

It happened with Guru Goraknath. He was an extremely enlightened man. Mohini and Maya are always the same, so you must realize what Mohini is.

It is the cosmic play. You can't get rid of it. But you can see that wherever I am, I am the same. God is reminding us all the time, lifetime after lifetime. You are not here just this lifetime. This lifetime we have karma together; therefore this lifetime again we are here.

It's so beautiful to be a human being. All human beings are divine; the whole creation is so beautiful. You have to feel. The more you feel, the more shining it will be, all the time shining. The more you churn cream, the more butter will come. (Laughing) What would you like to churn? Me? Do it! Do it! If God gives you somebody, churn! And you will surely get a result; there is no doubt! Even if I were a thousand miles away, I will be there.

In the same way, the more you feel that, the more you learn that this world is not eternal. Take a sankalpa for one day, for one week, for one month, to think that we are one. For one week, during every action you perform, remember that God is with you all the time even if many disturbances come. Choose a form, any form - Shree Maa, or Swamiji, or Kali, or Shiva. Take that form and think that they are with you all the time, and see how you feel. (Laughing) Just one week!

When pure consciousness is pulling you, when your mind is having pure consciousness, then I am there. That is "I Am." It is Me. When you have pure consciousness, then everything that comes to you is Truth. You will never make a mistake. It's beautiful! (Laughing) Keep that thought!

One day you finally knew
what you had to do, and began,
though the voices around you kept shouting
their bad advice -
though the whole house began to tremble
and you felt the old tug at your ankles.
"Mend my life!" each voice cried.
But you knew what you had to do,
though the wind pried with its stiff fingers,
at the very foundations,
though their melancholy was terrible.
But little by little as you left the voices behind,
the stars began to burn through the sheets of clouds,
there was a new voice which you slowly,
recognized as you own,
that kept you company,
as you strode deeper and deeper into the world.
Determined to do the only thing you could do -
determined to save the only life you could save.
- Mary Oliver

Shree Maa continues the interview:

In my whole life, I never slept. I'm praying all the time, twenty four hours a day. I have no sleep. I'm always on the subtle plane. Still now I'm always subtle. I love to have deep sleep. Sometimes when I leave my body, I go somewhere, but that's different. Then I say (in an excited voice) "I went deep today!" But that's very rare.

Recently, my blood pressure and pulse were high and they wanted to bring it down to normal. I went to the hospital and they gave me some medicine for a half hour and then one hour and my pulse never came down.

So I went back the next day. They gave me medicine and an IV. Normally one bottle of the IV would make somebody's pulse completely normal. They gave me one bottle, two bottles, three bottles, and my pulse didn't go down. They said, "This is a miracle. What should we do? I don't think her pulse will go down." The whole room and all the people were nervous and they said, "What is this?" Everyone was surprised and the radiologist was impressed and he wanted to come and visit me.

LIFE AFTER LIFE

Shree Maa:

There was never a time you weren't born. You have always been. There will never be a time when you will not be. With realization of infinite consciousness, your births are continuous - every moment is your birth.

Asked to explain further her comments about "This is one life," Shree Maa adds the following:

(Laughing) It's interesting, if you live inside yourself, the soul never dies and the soul is never born. It is all one thing. But if you count every lifetime, it's so many lives! For me, it's just one life.

(Laughing) I am doing the same thing lifetime after lifetime, but actually I feel it is just one life. You guys think, "Many lives" because you have so much karmic debt. Through every lifetime, you're trying to purify. But I am very conscious not to create any karma. I am very careful. Therefore, my life never changes.

I remember my previous lives, but I won't tell you. I don't talk about the past and I don't talk about future. I talk about the present. It's beautiful! Think about it! Is your life one lifetime, or many lifetimes? Think about it! Does it make sense?

This is the cycle of life. It's very subtle. That's why I said that you should finish any karma you started. If you don't do it right, you're borrowing karma and you will have to come back very soon and go around this world again. This is the world thread going, going, going (she draws concentric circles in the air) and after that it goes to the bindu.

Understand how we take birth lifetime after lifetime. On one side, it is beautiful. But, if you're attached to the world, you'll suffer.

Remember pure consciousness! That pure consciousness is God.

SALVATION

Friend, hope for the Teacher while you are alive.
Jump into experience while you are alive!
Thank ... and think ... while you are alive.
What you call "salvation" belongs to the time before death.
The idea that soul will rejoin with the ecstatic
Just because the body is rotten -
That is all fantasy.
What is found now is found then.
If you find nothing now,
you will simply end up with an apartment in the city of death.
So plunge into the truth, find out who the teacher is,
Believe in the great sound!
When the teacher is being searched for,
It is the intensity of the longing for the teacher
That does all the work.
- Kabir 16th Century Sufi Poet

Kabir's message calls for salvation now in the present and not in the distant future upon death. He rejects the common belief in most religions that a soul will automatically reach salvation upon death. Salvation requires one to plunge into the truth in the moment while alive and listen to the great sound. What is the truth? Who is the teacher and where is the great sound?

Shree Maa answers these questions in this interview.

Shree Maa:

In 1976, I was living in a devotee's house in Belur. Every night at the same time we had satsangha and one day, a young boy came. He was maybe seventeen or eighteen years old. I knew he had killed people and I told him I wouldn't give darshan now, but I would in the evening. My door was closed all day, and that boy was sitting in the other room, waiting for evening to come.

At evening arati time, when they gave me the charanamrita bowl (small bowl of yogurt, ghee and honey distributed as a prasad offering after arati), I saw an ant was swimming inside the charanamrita. I called the boy over using his name and he was surprised because he never told me his name.

Nobody knew that he had murdered people. I showed him the bowl where the ant was swimming, and asked him, "What's inside?" He said, "An ant." I said, "What would you like to do with it?" He replied, "I'd like to save it." So I said, "So why do you kill people?" and he was so surprised. I said, "You like to kill, so kill." He said, "I don't like to kill." "Why are you killing then? Promise me today you will never kill again."

For twenty minutes, he stood completely quiet. (Laughing) He became like a stone. After twenty minutes, I yelled, "Kill him or take it out and save him!"

Then he saved the ant from out of the charanamrita bowl. After that, the boy completely changed. He said, "I'm not going anywhere unless I'm with you all the time. Don't leave me." I told him, "I will never leave you, but you can't physically live with me, because I travel all over India and you need to study and get work. You have to do that."

My relationship with that boy was not one from a many lifetimes relationship; it was just some little karma. God sent him; God did work through me. So many people come and go, but some people stick with me, and then I know they are with me from past lives.

Later the boy's father came and hid him until the police were gone. I told the police and everybody else not to put him in jail; that he was going to be okay. That time in Calcutta was a very tough time. That was called the Nakshal period. The political situation made it horrible. During the Nakshal period they took young kids from their homes by force. The Nakshal people said, "If you don't give your boy to us, we'll kill you." The parents were afraid, and so they gave them their sons. It was a very tough period and for that reason the boy did what he did, he had to. I heard later that he got a job with the railway company.

Why did he come to me? Somebody told him, "Go there and she will save you." So he came to see me. There was a reason why he came. He was like Valmiki Muni[8]. Valmiki took care of his wife, father and mother. How? He was a gunda, a thief. Whoever went by his house, he would catch them and steal everything from them and sometimes, even kill them. He stole from people in order to take care of his family. That young boy who met me had no knowledge. When he got a little divine touch, he turned towards divinity. Same story.

---

8 See the story in the Reference Section.

VAISHANTI

In 1976, I moved to another house. It was a big colonial house. The British built these giant houses, and three hundred people could sit in the living room. One night I was doing arati in this house and a man came - he was the first man to come that day. Suddenly my head turned, and I looked at him and said, "Oooh! You came to investigate, huh?" He was surprised.

Before, I had written a letter to the West Bengal Chief Minister, Jyoti Basu, saying Ramakrishna told me to do a homa (fire ceremony) at Dakshineshwar. Jyoti Basu sent this man to be a spy and find out who wrote that letter. After that, all the other devotees started to come in. At that time I was always in samadhi, off and on, off and on.

That evening was very beautiful. After five or six hours my samadhi broke and lots of Chaitanya's shlokas (verses of poems by Chaitanya) came from my mouth. When I opened my eyes after reciting the shlokas, suddenly a name came out of my mouth, "Vaishanti! Where is Vaishanti?" Nobody answered. After two minutes, Vaishanti entered the room. I said, "Vaishanti!" She became scared and thought, "Why is she calling me?" I said, "Come over here, sit down with me." She was a very tall, beautiful lady, and she started to shake because this was the first time she ever saw me. She wondered, "How does she know my name is Vaishanti?"

She sat down with me, and I was stroking her hair, and I was falling in love with her (a mother's pure love for her child), and I said, "Vaishanti, how are you?" And she started to cry loudly. Everybody was surprised that she was crying so loudly. Then she told me her father was the Chief Minister of the State of Kashmir. When her father and mother got married, Swami Vivekananda told them, "If a daughter is born to you, give her the name, Vaishanti." So they gave her this Hindu name, but nobody knew that her secret name was Vaishanti because she is a Muslim. Only she, her mom and dad knew, so after a long time, when she heard me call her, "Vaishanti!" she started to cry.

After that, she became a great devotee. She's a lawyer and she established a school and took me to see it. She's now practicing in the Delhi High Court.

SEEING DUALITY FOR THE FIRST TIME

At that time my main focus was the Dakshineshwar homa. Ramakrishna had told me, "Do a homa for the world." India was having a tough time, as I was saying, it was during the Nakshal period.

There were a lot of young students around me, kids in their twenties who were great devotees. I said to them, "You guys organize everything at Dakshineshwar. Go to Dakshineshwar and find out if they will give us a place to do the homa." They eventually gave us a place in a field behind the fence where Ramakrishna's Kalpataru statue stands.

I invited four sadhus to perform the homa. Vashishta was one of them. For three months, all my Calcutta devotees collected wood, because there was going to be a big howan kund (fire pit), maybe fifty feet square. There were three trucks of wood: bilva wood, mango wood, sandal wood, and big drums of ghee. There were also thousands of lotus flowers. Everything was ready. From morning to morning the next day, thousands came to witness the homa.

Shree Maa performing the fire ceremony with devotees

One of the sadhus, the main pujari, was very negative. Everything was ready, but he said he wouldn't do the homa. All the devotees said to him, "You have to do it!" and he was a little scared, so he did it.

At three o'clock in the afternoon, I was in samadhi at the Kalpataru temple. I woke up and two sadhus came to me and said, "Mother, we can't dig the howan kund! The ground is too hard. If we can't dig, we can't do the homa." Now the homa was to start that night at eight o'clock. I knew that twelve after eight was an auspicious time.

Suddenly two men appeared. They had dark colored identical short pants. These two men said, "Mother, we can dig your howan kund." I didn't know them! Within half an hour, they dug the howan kund. When they finished their task, they disappeared! Isn't that something? You can see how God is taking care of everything.

At twelve after eight we started the fire. And from eight thirty to three a.m. there was a homa. It was a big fire! There was a big ghee spoon with a long handle, and Vashishta was pouring the ghee into the fire. Thousands of people offered masala. One of my devotees, Purnima, was so overwhelmed with bhava (spiritual emotion), that she had a vision of the Divine Mother and she fainted.

When the homa was finished, the sadhu who had originally refused to do the homa wanted to show his own power. He had a clay pot with some cow dung in it, and he threw in frankincense and ghee. This made a big fire within the little clay pot. He held that scalding pot in his hands, but he didn't get burned. After that he put the pot in other people's hands and their hands didn't burn and he said, "See your hand isn't burning." He was showing off. He wanted to show people he was a big, powerful sadhu.

Another sadhu got up and came to me and said, "Mother, I'm going to break that pot!" (Laughing) I was surprised and I thought, "What's going on?" On one side, I was completely detached, and on another side I was interested in watching their play.

The second sadhu got up, and he started doing mantras. Right away the pot broke down the middle! And the other sadhu got so mad! I was thinking, "My God, what is this lila?" There were thousands of people and they were getting impressed with these sadhus.

The first sadhu created another fire in another clay pot and the second sadhu said some mantras and broke that pot too! Again the first sadhu made a pot, and again the second sadhu broke it with his mantras!

After that, I stood up, and I told the first sadhu, "You be quiet. This is not a competition. This homa was created to invite God here and to make peace."

After that, I heard that sadhu suffered a lot. I decided I will never invite any sadhu to do a homa. I did not after that until I met Swami Satyananda. You can see that the first sadhu was doing what he was doing with ego. The second sadhu had a true power and he used it for good. He was performing the homa with great devotion and when he saw what the first sadhu was doing, he wanted to break his ego. He thought, "Mother is here, why are you trying to show your power and ego?" He showed his ego at a perfect time.

I thought sadhus always lived in truth. When these two sadhus let their egos compete with each other, I realized that some sadhus lived in duality and were not completely surrendered to God. It really opened my eyes. I never saw this kind of thing before. I knew that duality was all around in this world, but I was never conscious of it. This was the first day duality was in my consciousness.

I never felt duality because I was in higher consciousness all the time. Everything was divine. I was completely in my own world. I was living with Ramakrishna all the time. So I realized I shouldn't expect that every sadhu would be Ramakrishna! (Laughing) I thought God was saying to me, "Hey, Maa, it's not only your world!"

God showed me that it is not only non-duality in this world. I have to see duality also. It's like watching a play. It was really beautiful to see how the world dances. I was completely out of the dance. Yeah, (sighing) I never felt like I was living in duality. When I came to America, I felt I was living with duality and non-duality. It started slowly and took about a year.

(Laughing) I understand it's hard to have pure love in this country. I'm very sad to see this, you know. I love all my children here, but they are so poor. They are poor even though this country is very rich. We're concerned with how to make money, how to be a big man; mostly name, fame, gain and competition.

Jesus gave us knowledge, but how many people are following this knowledge? His main seed was pure love. How many really follow pure love? Selfish attachment is everywhere.... Sometimes I feel sad that you guys have to work this hard because you're so involved in maya.

I am the Mother. If you are sad I feel, "Oh my child is suffering, I'd like to cure him." All mothers feel that. But I am not attached to the feeling. I'd like to take away their suffering, but I can't always do that because they have to experience their own karma. But I will give a blessing! I will give good advice. If you accept the advice, you will learn quickly, and then there will be no more suffering. By experiencing your karma and learning from it you can get rid of your suffering.

After people enjoy their materialism, maybe they'll want to study wisdom! (Laughing) Some people are trying really, really hard to change, and some people are trying only a little bit.

FULFILLING PREVIOUS KARMA

A conscious soul in the unconscious world,
Hidden behind our thoughts and hopes and dreams,
An indifferent Master singing Nature's acts
Leaves the vicegerent's mind a seeming king.
In his floating house upon the sea of time
The regent sits at work and never rests;
He is a puppet of the dance of the time;
He is driven by the hours, the moment's call
Compels him with the thronging of life's need
And the babels of the voices of the world
- Savitri, Book II

A soul is immortal and will always remain the same throughout eternity. However, when a soul departs from the body, shedding character traits and memories on its way to its resting place, the soul carries with it the essence of its past experiences and not the details. The essence of the past experience helps (or hinders) in the growth towards the divine. That is why ordinary people have no physical memory of outward events and circumstances of past lives. For a highly evolved person like Shree Maa, where a soul is in constant contact with consciousness and it records within itself external forms, words and sounds. In this way, the subtle physical remains in a seed memory for highly evolved souls, which emerges in their next lives.

In this interview, Shree Maa shares how memories from her previous life take on new expressions and actions for the work that had to be done, always for the Divine.

THE RAMESHWARAM TEMPLE

Shree Maa:

One day I said, "Hey! I'd like to go to Rameshwaram tomorrow!" Everybody knew I was a crazy Mother. Who knows what she's going to say next? Joydeep, K. N. Parvat and a couple of women got tickets that evening and the next morning we went to Rameshwaram.

I told all the devotees, "Please, everybody bring some bilvapatra leaves and write 'Sri Ram' on them with sandal paste." The bilvapatra is a special leaf for Shiva. They wrote 'Sri Ram' on 108 leaves and we took them all to Rameshwaram. It was so great!

I was on a horse cart on the road to Rameshwaram and suddenly, I said to the driver, "Hey Ganesh! Take me down that road!" Ganesh was surprised and thought (laughing), "How does she know my name?" So we went down the road and there, right in front of us, was an elephant. In a previous lifetime I knew that elephant, that's why I went down that road.

I got down from the cart, and I stood in front of him, and you wouldn't believe it, but he started to cry. He put his trunk on my head, as if he was hugging me with his trunk!

109

Joydeep and K. N. Parvat started to cry too! Then I fed him.

Then we went to the Rameshwaram temple to do puja. The main priest, who was eighty years old, brought out a big fat book. When you do puja there, you write your name in the book. Every big temple in South India does that and you can see if your previous generations came there.

The priest told us that in the morning we should go to the twenty-one kunds at Rameshwaram. A kund is a kind of well. At each of the twenty-one kunds you take a bath. After that, you go to the ocean and take a bath, and after that you come back to the temple for the main puja. The priest told us the puja would cost five thousand rupees. When he said that, K.N. Parvat fainted. K.N. is a pure man and he knew the priest was corrupt.

K.N. is a big man and he completely fell down. The priest started to chant mantras to wake him up, but even after a long time, he wasn't getting anywhere. By then it was eleven at night and Joydeep realized the priest was useless.

I was in the other room with some devotees, and at eleven o'clock Joydeep came in and said to me, "Mother, you have to do something. K.N. is not waking up!" I touched K.N.'s forehead and he woke up. He looked around and then he said, "Mother, my puja is done! Let's go back tomorrow!"

After that, the priest became really humble, "I'll do whatever you want." Next day, everyone went to the twenty-one kunds, and I gave a bath to everybody. After the ocean bath, we came back.

When we returned, the priest was ready with a band and the elephant. They took me to the front of the procession, and the whole band party followed with the elephant. Isn't that nice? The whole Rameshwaram Temple joined in the procession.

After that, we did a special puja and I gave the hundred and eight bilva leaves to another priest, who did puja. He was very old. It was such a beautiful darshan of Shiva that day! No one can enter inside, only the priest can perform the puja, so we were sitting in front.

When I gave the hundred and eight bilvapatra leaves to the priest, he started to cry saying, "Nobody has ever done that!" "Nobody has ever thought to write, Sri Ram, Sri Ram on so many leaves!" He looked at me and said, "Mother Sarada came with gold leaves, and you came with green leaves with the name Sri Ram!" He realized who I was.

When we were about to leave the Rameshwaram Temple, I wanted to see the elephant again and I took a mala to him. They had put him in a cage. When the elephant saw me, he started running towards me! He ran and he stuck his trunk through a little hole in the cage, and he took my mala, and he put it on his head. Isn't that beautiful? After that I said, "My karma is done."

KARMA IS SUBTLE

You know, karma is very subtle. Even little things create karma. Even when you say you're going to do something and you don't do it, you're creating karma. If you made dinner, and you didn't clean up completely after yourself, and someone had to clean up for you, then you are creating karma. If not for this life, maybe for your next lifetime. That's why we say, "Be efficient" and respect your actions all the time. When we respect our actions all the time, we are not creating any karma. Therefore, even as a child I never gave orders to the servants who were around me all the time. They said they didn't understand me because I never gave them orders, even for a glass of water. I always did it myself.

If someone said to the servants, "Get me some water," that person is giving orders to them and creating karma. Therefore I teach everybody, "Never give orders." Instead say, "Could you do a favor for me?"

Be conscious of everything in every moment. When you remain conscious in every moment, consciousness is always with you. That's why we want people to do sadhana. Doing sadhana is the way to become conscious all the time. When you respect your actions all the time, it's your sadhana, it's your puja and it's your meditation.

DIVINE PLAY

I think God might be a little prejudiced.
For once He asked me to join Him
on a walk through this world,
and we gazed into every heart on this earth,
and I noticed he lingered a little bit longer
before any face that was weeping,
and before any eyes that were laughing.
And sometimes when we passed a soul in worship
God too would kneel down.
I have come to learn: God adores His creation.
- Saint Francis of Assisi

Shree Maa, devoid of any traces of individual self, embodies universal SELF and adores God's creation and loves every one. She responds differently to different people, depending on their spiritual maturity and material desires. Her actions are different ways to teach people and remind them they are Gods who have forgotten who they really are. She is always a kind mother to all; some times she plays with her devotees, sometimes she tests, sometimes she challenges, other times she fulfills their deepest desires. The purpose that motivates everything she does, is to wake people up, so they can realize their greatest potential.

She picked up the story after the Dakshineshwar homa:

I went to many different places spreading love. It was heaven! During that time, Gautam, one of my devotees, was begging me to initiate him, but I wasn't giving initiation at that time in my life. He insisted, "Mother, you have to give me initiation!" I said, "Listen, until Thakur tells me to, I can't give initiation. Go to Belur Math and take initiation there. That's my place also."

He was such a naughty boy, you know. Generally, at midday, I did arati behind closed doors, and nobody could stay in my temple then. One day, I was doing arati, and suddenly, Gautam snuck up and touched my feet! At that time nobody could touch my body.

Here in America I gave up lots of things because of the culture. In India I never did puja in front of people. When I did puja, my door was always closed. Swamiji told me we have to show people here how to be divine.

In India I didn't even eat in front of anybody. If people came to me for darshan and they had a certain kind of stone (for an astrological remedy), I wouldn't give darshan until they took it off. I felt that if instead of praying to God they wore a stone, it showed a lack of faith in God.

After being here ten years, I went back to India, and there were thousands of people crying. For five days they cried, "Why has our Mother changed?" Now I don't tell anybody I'm coming to India, just a few devotees. It's very hard for me because so many people cry because they don't want me to leave. In Delhi they brought guards for me. Nowadays, if I go, I may stay seven days, and just see a few devotees that I call when I get there.

So you can see that when Gautam touched my feet, it was a big deal. I started spinning. I didn't know where I was. I was spinning, spinning, and I fell down. After I fell down, I couldn't walk by myself anymore. I couldn't walk for one month, so I stayed in bed. There were so many doctors and nurses who were devotees and they couldn't find anything wrong. They couldn't do anything. Gautam was crying, crying, crying. He gave up his job! He was constantly coming to see me and crying.

A young girl was doing seva to me all the time. Her name was Bona and she was fourteen years old and very pure. On a new moon day I told her, "If you can spend twenty-four hours without drinking one drop of water, then you can touch my body while reciting mantra." She was so sweet, she didn't drink one drop of water and then she touched my body with devotion while she recited mantra. The next day I could walk.

God was giving a teaching. When you really love God, like the young girl did, your selfish desires go away. At that time, you are God. You and I are not separate, do you understand?

On the other hand, Gautam acted selfishly and God showed him who I was. Gautam had his own selfish desires and because of the demands he was making on me, God showed that form.

Krishna went to Dhritarashtra's court to make peace and prevent a war. Krishna said, "We don't want to fight, please give back the kingdom of Indraprashta to Yudhisthira and we won't have a war." Duryodhana told Him, "I will never give back Indraprashta!" The second time Krishna came he said, "OK, if you won't give back Indraprashta, then give just five villages." But Duryodhana wouldn't even give five villages. Then Krishna showed his

Vishvarupa, his Divine form, but Duryodhana continued to insult Krishna. He said, "Kick this cow herd out!"

Krishna showed his real form and it didn't affect Duryodhana. Because of his impurity, he couldn't see Krishna's form. There were four pure people there who saw it. The impure people saw only light, which made them blind.

This is true also in our relationship. Everybody has some kind of Duryodhana nature, selfish desire. Every individual has selfish desires, which make them unhappy and prevents them from seeing divinity.

A POOR DEVOTEE'S DESIRE IS FULFILLED

I stayed in Calcutta for a long time. I had so many devotees there and I started teaching puja house to house. It was an incredible time. I would tell a devotee, "Chant the Ramayana for twenty-four hours," and they did. How devoted they were!

In the evening devotees came and sang for me. Sometimes they sang all night long, and then they went to their jobs in the morning. When I was in samadhi, they meditated with me and never moved. They forgot their children; they forgot their families. I would wake up at three o'clock in the morning, and everybody was meditating. It was a wonderful, wonderful time!

At that house one day a servant watched me and bowed down to me from far away. She was thinking, "Mother goes to so many places, and so many people come to see Mother. I wish Mother would go to my house, but I am very poor. Mother would never come to my house." The next day I told Bona, "I would like to go to that woman's house, but in secret. Don't tell anybody!" She told me, "Mother, she isn't home. Why would you like to go now?" I said (laughing),

"Because that's the time I need to go - when she isn't home!"

Bona took me to the maidservant's house. She lived in the servant's quarters and had five children. When we went to her house, there was a three year old baby at home. First I went to her kitchen, and I touched the food and ate a little bit. I did it to make her happy (because I blessed the food and made it prasad). Later when the maidservant came home in the evening, she went to the kitchen and saw some food had been eaten. She wondered, "What's happened?" The next day she asked Bona, "You know, my son told me somebody came to my house and ate food. We don't know who it was." Bona told her, "Meditate and think about who came to your house! You will find out," but she still couldn't figure it out. After one week, she discovered that I went there and she cried and cried.

Her elder son was a rickshaw wallah. She told him he should be present all the time to take me here and there. How devoted!

THE SEWER MAN

Every day that I would go out, another man would bow down to me from far away. He cleaned the sewage system. In India he was an untouchable. One day he was standing with many other people in a field and I walked up to him. He was eating betel leaves and I took some from his mouth and I started to chew. He cried. I hugged him and all the people started to cry. He became a great devotee. It changed his life because at that moment he realized that God has no caste, that God is the universe.

Love has no caste; God has no caste. Everything is God's creation. This sewer man, the maidservant, their pure love was calling me. When pure love is calling God, God is present every time. Pure love can touch God very quickly.

Shree Maa wanted to include here the following story that Ramakrishna liked to tell:

There were two friends who met while walking along a path. They came to a temple where spiritual dialogues were taking place. One friend said, "Come, my friend, let us hear the word of God." His friend looked surprised and declined, saying that he had a date with a prostitute. Thus the two friends parted, one to visit the temple and the other to enjoy himself with his lady friend.

But after a short time of sexual dalliance, the one man said to himself, "My friend is sitting in the temple listening to the word of God, while I'm indulging my sexual desires. Certainly I am a fool." At the same time the friend, who was sitting in the temple listening to spiritual talks, thought to himself, "Boy, am I a fool! My friend is enjoying the company of that prostitute, while I'm listening to these dull speeches."

When death came, the man who was with the prostitute, but yearned for God went directly to heaven. God doesn't look at where you are, but at what quality of mind you have when you are there. God receives the expressions of the heart. God acts differently according to the time and place.

For example, Krishna acted a certain way when he was baby Gopal. When he was older and living with Yashoda, he acted differently. When he came back to Mathura, he was different again. He acted differently each time for a particular purpose. That is our play. One can't say, "Mother is a Divine Being. Why isn't she doing the same things Krishna did?"

You had a question when you first met me; you were confused. You thought, (she says this in a funny way and I know she's joking with me), "She looks like a simple woman, she doesn't feel like a guru." You saw only one part of me. You had a thought about how a guru should act. You didn't see the whole universe. This is human life.

Shankaracharya was a great pundit. One day he took a bath in the Ganges and as he was coming back, he saw a dirty man with many dogs in his path. He said (Shree Maa speaks loudly, impersonating Shankaracharya), "Hey! Get out from my way!" The man said, "Ooh! You think that I'm untouchable! You give so many lectures about Vedanta, and still the soul is untouchable? If I touch you, will you be untouchable?" Then Shankaracharya said to himself, "Yes, he's making sense. What am I doing?" Then that dirty man changed form and became Shiva.

A NEW DEVOTEE IS TESTED

I was visiting many devotees and making temples in their homes, like I'm doing in America. One day a lady wanted to see me. She was a head nurse in a hospital and a worldly woman. She heard from somebody that Mother came, and she wanted to see me, but whatever day she came, I locked the door. I would not give her darshan.

Because she didn't have a true feeling inside; she was just curious. On the first day, when I kept her out, the gate was locked, and when she left she felt a little bit of devotion, a little desire was created. When she came the next day and the door was locked, I was inside, intuitively working with her. She came a third day and I still didn't give her darshan. On the fourth day, I went to her house with Bona. I knew she was working and wasn't there.

Oh, my God, her house was really dirty! There was no altar there, no God there. Gopal was sitting on a little, dirty shelf. I knew I would see that. We cleaned the room and made a beautiful altar. We set up everything and left. The lady came back from her job, and she was surprised, "What happened? Who came? Who did this?" She said to the maidservant, "Did you do this?" The servant said, "No, no. A woman came and she did it." The lady asked, "Which woman?" The servant said, "I don't know. (Laughing) I thought she was a relative."

She thought about this day after day. Finally, she came to see me and my gate was closed again. I was watching her. Within two weeks, she changed completely. On the next full moon day she knew the altar had been created by me. She had been praying for that. Then she came, and at that time I gave her darshan and she became a great devotee. And that devotee's name is Purnima! After she met me, she didn't want to leave. I stayed at her house a long time. We had satsanghas at her house and the whole hospital staff: doctors, nurses, workers, all started to come to see me.

With Purnima I was traveling a lot all over India. Purnima worked for the railway; and I had a free first class ticket as her mother! (Laughing) I am her mother! I went all over India.

GO TO MADURAI!

One devotee's mother was a bank manager, and she was very greedy. Her husband was sick, half-paralyzed and living in Madurai, but she wasn't going to see him. I thought, "I need to change her."

One day, I made fish, meat and eggs for her and fed her. I said, "You have to go to Madurai to see your husband!" I made her go by force. She took the train from Assam to Calcutta; from there she was to go to Madurai. She decided to stop at Purnima's house in Calcutta on the way. I was staying there too.

I told every one that I have to go to Dakshineshwar, and before going, I cooked vegetarian food for her. I told her, "You stay here; you can't go with me." While I was gone, she ate the vegetarian food, and while eating, she told Purnima in a loud voice, "She doesn't want to feed me fish any more!" She was complaining about me.

Then, as she was eating, underneath the rice, a little fish appeared. The lady said, "She's a tricky woman! She likes to play games with me!" When I came back, I said, "How many days will you do this? If you're not pure, I'll play games with you! Go to Madurai now!" Siva had told me her husband had only five days left. Her husband died five days after she got to Madurai.

CONNECTION WITH GURU

When a guru really gives initiation to somebody, the guru never leaves that person until the disciple is liberated. If a disciple remembers me, we stay together even after death. (Laughing) This is one soul. Your karma goes. It doesn't matter, good or bad. It's going when you are doing something unconsciously, and you are not aware that it is ego. If you knew this is my ego, then you wouldn't do it. If you know you are doing bad, that's different.

(Laughing) But the guru always protects, there is no question about that. When a disciple will be in bhava (without any worldly distraction) all the time and he will work detached. Like that one song, (Shree Maa sings):
Jayre name prashatara, kati bol,
Tapu jvala chovana
Radhe bol, bari bol,

120

bhaing jana kari bol,
doga hare choghana!
Inside the water, I'm swimming,
but the water isn't touching me.
I'm cooking and I'm offering it to everybody,
but I'm not touching the pot!
Cooking, but I'm not touching.

Do you know the meaning? (Laughing) Yeah. (Laughing) You have to be like that. Always remember, we came to this world to play. We have to be good actors. Yeah, I love to play a part. Yes! It's a funny world. It's a beautiful world, if you really know this world.

You don't know where I'm living while I'm here. I'm the boat; you guys are the water. I'm floating and sometimes I go under the water and then I come back. I'm unattached. If God has a real devotee for me, they will come to me and do God's work. You understand? It's not hard at all; it's beautiful. But the ego is very tricky - the ego comes up quickly.

When you realize you did wrong, that is sadhana also. But what will I say? This is all drama. I can tell you to be true, be pure and love God - that's all. We came alone and we'll go alone. Why not love God and be true? Why not? Worldly attachments will not take you to heaven.

WEDDING BLESSING

It was so beautiful when I went to Benares. I went to the Annapurna Temple for the first time. When I saw the Annapurna Mother at the temple, I fainted. It was so beautiful! A big light came from Mother, and that light made me faint. Since then Annapurna has always been very important to me. All the devotees protected me for several

121

hours while I lay on the temple floor. Many people came to this temple and I was in the middle, but nobody moved me because of all the devotees surrounding me. The priests were upset and were saying bad things.

When I got a little consciousness, I was talking with the inner Mother. She said, "I will give you a garland, and then you'll wake up." Then a pundit came over to me, and he gave me a garland from Annapurna and then I woke up. Isn't that beautiful? What a beautiful connection!

Before going into the temple the next day, I took a handful of rice with me. I knew that somebody would prevent me from going inside the temple. As I entered the temple, a lady stood in front of me and said, "I won't allow you to go inside the temple unless you give me something." I gave the rice to her and I went inside. I think she saw me when I was unconscious in the temple.

Later that lady explained to me that her daughter was getting married, but they were very poor. She said the rice I gave her made food for five hundred people! Automatically everything came for her daughter's marriage and everything went smoothly. She became a great devotee afterwards.

GOD IS EVERYWHERE

God spoke to me,
"I want all souls to consummate with me,
so I devised a plan:
As each soul nears me,
All differences will dissolve,
to such a sublime extent
that when the heart looks upon any object in this world
it will cry 'Beloved'
and passionately run into an embrace with me,"
That blessed grace I now know.
I now see my Beloved everywhere.
-Saint John of the Cross

There are a thousand ways of approaching and realizing the Divine within and each way has its own experiences. We believe that Shree Maa's way is for one to surrender his or her own self unconditionally to the Divine, turning it away from the external things and towards the Divine. The reason we use the word "We believe" is because she does not preach, but we see her living it every day, every hour and every second. For some of us who need proof that the Divine within can be realized, she provides it with a certainty that this self-transformation is possible and this realization is possible.

In our last talk Shree Maa told the story of how she fainted in the Benares Annapurna temple after having had a vision of Mother Annapurna. She picks up the story after returning from Benares.

Shree Maa:
After we went to the Annapurna temple, we came back to Calcutta and were there for a long time. I was teaching everyone puja and meditation. One day I knew a sadhu was going to come to see me from a different city, so I locked myself up in the house for three days. Nobody could see me; nobody could touch me. On the day the sadhu came, I

told some devotees to chant continuously and other devotees to read the Ramayana continuously. I told one of my devotees named Dhamaru, "Today will be a really good play."

On the third day, at four in the afternoon, I opened my door and the sadhu arrived. He was a practitioner of tantra vidya. I went into samadhi, but I heard later from the devotees that he brought lots of bones, human bones and skulls, and said many different mantras. At the time I was very young (early twenties) and these sadhus were older. In West Bengal, they had never seen anyone like me at such a young age. They wondered, "Is she the real thing?"

I woke up around eleven thirty at night and I saw the sadhu sitting there. Dhamaru was getting so mad, and he started to attack him. I said, "Stop, Dhamaru." He said, "Mother, you don't know what he did to you!" Then the sadhu said, "Mother, I did whatever I've learned to you, and now I'd like to do puja to you." I asked him, "What did you do?" He said, "I tried to wake you up with my many different vidyas." He wanted to have some effect, but he saw nothing happened. So after that, he did puja to me, bowed down and left. Ultimately, he became a good devotee.

There are three types of sadhus: rajoguna, tamoguna, and sattvaguna. I was sattvaguna, and he was tamoguna and rajoguna. At Kurukshetra there were two armies: Duryodhana's and the Pandavas'. The Pandavas lived with truth and dharma and Duryodhana's army was adharmic. On the Pandavas' side were just a couple of kings and Krishna. On Duryodhana's side was most of India, most of the kings, and millions of soldiers. But the Pandavas won the war. It always happens this way.

I saw that not all sadhus are about Truth. Mostly they're rajoguna and tamoguna sadhus. They learn a little bit, and then they show their power. They can't get anywhere.

That event also opened my eyes a little bit. From my childhood I never lived without Truth. I saw that this world also had these things and I thought, "OK, fine."

VASHISHTA'S DEVOTION

After that Vashishta wanted to take me to his house at Durga Puja time to do puja to me. Vashishta was a great devotee. Vashishta's altar was on the east side of his house and he wanted to move it to the north side. He said he wanted to do puja to me before he moved his altar.

I was doing arati with lotus flowers three times a day for Navaratri: morning, midday, and evening. One morning I asked Vashishta, "Where is my lotus flower?" Vashishta said, "Mother, I didn't get any lotus flowers today."

Vashishta was worried, "Where can I find a lotus flower now? The bazaars are closed. I don't want to disappoint Mother."

Then he went to take a bath in a little pond he had in his back yard. Brahmins have a rule that they go under the water three times while saying the Gayatri mantra. After he went under the third time, he came out, and in his hand was a lotus flower. He ran back to the house crying. They still have that lotus flower, which they keep very nicely on the altar.

Vashishta was crying the whole day, saying, "Mother, how many times will you play with me?" (Laughing) Here is a very good example of devotion. Vashishta is extremely devoted: he loves God, he loves Mother and he loves me. Whenever you have completely pure love, God fulfills your desires. That day this truth was shown to everybody.

Vashishta was a pure devotee, and he thought, "Mother wants a lotus flower" and with his pure devotion, he got a lotus flower. It appeared! It is so beautiful; your pure devotion can do anything. Pure devotion can melt stone, too.

After that, Vashishta did puja to me. He washed my feet with the five offerings of charanamrita: milk, yogurt, honey, sugar and ghee. Then when it was time to take the plate from under my feet, it wouldn't come out. It wouldn't detach from my feet. My feet were stuck to it.

I was in samadhi and I didn't know anything. He did the puja at eleven o'clock in the morning and I came back at seven in the evening. They waited all that time for Mother to wake up and for the plate to come out from under my feet. The time was drawing close to when he was supposed to move the altar. (Laughing) Then I woke up and he moved the altar.

That day Mother Kali was dancing! Everywhere there was a beautiful smell, everywhere there was a pleasant air; everyone was completely in bhava. Everywhere jiva, we call the five-element body jiva, and atman were completely lovey-dovey.

To have that, we need tapasya (spiritual practice and detachment from the desires of the world). With tapasya we can get everything and you will be with everything.

THE QUEEN AND THE SEWER MAN

In West Bengal, there once was a king whose queen was extremely beautiful. The queen and king were very dharmic. The queen had a favorite servant, whose husband cleaned the toilets and sewers of the city.

One day the queen went to the Ganges and the servant's husband saw her. He was stunned by her beauty. When her husband went home, he was completely quiet because he was constantly thinking of the queen. His wife said to him, "What happened? Are you sick?" but he wouldn't answer. He stopped going to work and he didn't eat. He just sat and stared.

The wife went to the queen and told her about her husband. The queen was very intelligent and said, "Tell him the queen wants to know what happened, and then maybe I can help him resolve his problem." (Laughing) The servant went home and told her husband, "The queen wants to know what happened so she can try to help solve your problem." As soon as she said, "the queen can try to help solve your problem," he said, "Really!" She said, "Tell me what happened to you," and then he told her.

The wife went back and told the queen, "You're the problem!" (Laughing) The servant explained what had happened and said her husband would like to see the queen again. The queen said, "I'm going on a certain day to offer food to all the sadhus. He should come there wearing sadhu's clothes, and very loudly recite the mantra, 'Tara! Tara! Tara!' Then I will recognize him."

So the sewer man went to see the queen wearing sadhu's clothes, and sat down with all the sadhus, constantly reciting, "Tara! Tara! Tara! Tara!" He tried to act like a real sadhu.

The more he chanted "Tara," the more he enjoyed it, until by the time the queen came before him, he was completely absorbed in the mantra. The queen offered food to him, but he didn't seem to notice her. He bowed down to the queen, left home, and went into the jungle to be a sadhu.

Sometimes if you pretend, it becomes real. It's hard to see everybody as Ramakrishna. We are constantly reacting to other people's actions. If a delivery man would come right now, it would be very hard to see him as Ramakrishna (laughing) because he acts and looks different from Ramakrishna. Therefore tapasya is needed. With tapasya you won't get attached to or deluded by others' actions.

Look inside anyone and see your Guru there. Everybody is good inside. If you see their purity, sometimes they will change. For example, at your job you're trying to see the pure soul inside your client. Before you never looked at that pure soul; you looked at the outside. Sometimes you fell in love with them; sometimes you didn't like them. (Laughing) When you see correctly your aversion will not come, your selfish love will not come; only pure love will come.

If you are looking at that person inside in a pure way, then I am there. I am there. When you're looking for purity, impurity will not come to you; not at all. You will be completely calm and quiet. When a doctor does his duty with the divine in his heart, gives his advice with the divine in his heart, the people get cured. That's the way it works. That's what people call a miracle. It's no miracle; it's just the divine work.

From the beginning of my life
I have been looking for your face, but today I have seen it.
Today I have seen the charm, the beauty,
the unfathomable grace of the face that I was looking for.
Today I found you,
And those who laughed and scorned me yesterday
Are sorry they were not looking as I did.
I am bewildered by the magnificence of your beauty
And wish to see you with a hundred eyes.
My heart has burned with passion and has searched
For ever for this wondrous beauty that I know behold.
Your fragrant breath, like the morning breeze has come
to the stillness of the garden.
You have breathed new life into me.
I have become your sunshine and also your shadow.
My soul is screaming in ecstasy,
Every fiber of my being in love with you.

Your effulgence has lit a fire in my heart.
You have made radiant for me the earth and the sky
My arrow of love has arrived at the target
I am in the house of mercy and my heart is a blaze of prayer.
-Rumi

Previously Shree Maa talked about how Vashishta's devotion had manifested a lotus flower. Shree Maa began this interview in her usual happy mood.

Shree Maa:

I lived at Vashishta's house for a long time and we had satsangha every day. Many devotees came from far away. Most of the time I was in samadhi. These people had so many worldly attachments, but when they saw me in samadhi, they sat down and meditated. They didn't think, "I have to go back home," they completely dissolved. They were so absorbed in meditation that they couldn't move. When I woke up, they woke up. Sometimes I would wake up at around three a.m. and when I opened my eyes, I saw all the devotees sitting there, meditating. In the morning they left to go to their jobs.

How beautiful they were, how devoted they were! They forgot family, friends, everything. It was a beautiful time. What can we learn from that? Every human being is a form of God. When a human being is touched by that spirit, they realize that we are one soul. When they meet a pure soul, they wake up.

Every human being can do that! These devotees were worldly people. They had children, families, jobs to go to everyday. They had many attachments, but they came to see me, and they dissolved.

Then I went with Vashishta and other devotees to the Kamakhya temple and I also went to the cremation grounds in Gauhati to meditate. At the cremation grounds there is a feeling of detachment. When you watch all the bodies burning, you feel completely detached. You realize that this world is not eternal. Your spirit wakes up; you have no fear. You conquer fear and that's a very great thing. I was born near a cremation ground and passed by it every day.

MOTHER SARADA COMES IN A DREAM

Then we came back to Gauhati. One day a woman came from another city. Her husband saw me - saw Sarada Devi - in a dream, and was told by Ramakrishna to go and see me. Ramakrishna told him, "Go there and see Mother." He wanted to find out if it was true that Mother was really there. The husband couldn't walk; he was half-paralyzed, so he told his wife, "Go to this place. Mother Sarada is sitting there, I need to see her."

His wife came and saw me, and said, "My husband told me about you. I don't know who you are, but you have to come with me." The husband had explained everything to her, including where I was living. I knew she would come.

I went with her and saw her husband and we both recognized each other and he cried. After that, I became bound by his pure love. He was extremely pure and very devoted to Thakur. I stayed there many days, and did tapasya with him, teaching him. I established Shiva at their house and he started to chant the Chandi and different mantras. We had a wonderful time.

Wherever I went at that time of my life, when I sat down in samadhi, everyone went into samadhi, into deep meditation with me. This went on day after day, month after month, with hundreds of people. The whole city came to know me at that time. So much was happening in people's lives; I can't explain it to you.

GIVING KALI A LIFT

Mahavir was a great devotee of Ramakrishna; he didn't do anything without his Guru. All the time he was talking about Ramakrishna and singing about Ramakrishna. One day I went to Kalapahar from my house and Mahavir wanted to go too. It was hard to get there and we had to take a rickshaw and a bus. On the way back we came to the bus station very late at night, about eleven o'clock, and there was no taxi, no cars, and no rickshaw. We were stuck and unable to do anything.

Mahavir saw a jeep with a man sitting in it and he went to him and said, "My Maa is with us, could you give us a lift?" Right away, the man said, "Yes, I'll give you a lift." Isn't that great? He took us to Mahavir's house, dropped us off, and he left. We didn't know anything about him.

Early in the morning, at three thirty, a knocking on the door was heard. At that time, I was in samadhi. Mahavir said, "It's early in the morning! Who's knocking at the door?" Mahavir opened the door, and saw the man who gave us a lift and he said, "Where is Mother? Last night you wanted a lift for Mother, where is that Mother? I had a dream and Mother Kali said to me, 'You left Me, and you didn't see Me.'"

Mahavir asked him, "Where did you come from?" The man said, "I came from Kamakhya." The man was a government contractor and everybody called him Bhaiti. He came and sat down with me, and was crying, crying, crying. After that he became a great devotee. He promised that whatever I needed, he would take care of it, and everyday he came to see me and meditate with me.

SHREE MAA COMES TO SWAMI'S TEMPLE

Then I went back to Kamakhya and at full moon time, I offered Mother a hundred and eight ghee lights. In my meditation, I saw a man come from heaven, reciting the Devi Shuktam (a song of praise to the Divine Mother from the Chandi). He was a foreign man and he merged with Rudra, the Shiva in the Kamakhya temple. Then I heard Mother tell me, "You have to meet Satya; you have to meet Satyananda." I woke up, and told everybody.

Before that lots of names came when I was in samadhi and then those people came to see me. I said, "Who is Satya? Do you know anybody named Satya?" Mahavir laughed and answered, "Oh Mother! He will come to you, don't worry!"

Once again while I was meditating I heard Mother's voice, "You have to go to Bakreshwar, and you have to meet Satya." Again I woke up and told everybody, "Mother told me I have to go to Bakreshwar. Where is Bakreshwar?" Mahavir said, "Oh, I know Bakreshwar, it's in West Bengal. There's a Mother's Shakti Pith (a famous Divine Mother temple) there." I said, "I have to go there and meet Satya."

Within two days we left. At that time I was crazy, you know, flying everywhere, at any time. It didn't matter if it was two or three in the morning. Everyone knew that's the way I acted.

I went to the Sunrise School in Howrah that was owned by Joydeep, and we took a school bus without telling anyone! I didn't care, because I needed to go. (Laughing) So many devotees went with me to Bakreshwar, which was far away, more than seven hours by bus! (Laughing) We stayed at a hotel near Shiva's temple.

I did Mother's puja at that Shakti Pith, then I went to another temple dedicated to Mother Kali, Ramakrishna and Sarada Devi. I sat down at that temple and I went into samadhi, and suddenly, after a couple of hours of sitting still, energy pulled me. I got up and started running. (Laughing) The energy was taking me, and everyone was running behind me.

Suddenly I stopped at a small ashram named Ramakrishna Tapo Math. A brahmachari was opening the locked gate to the temple. I said to him, "Hey, I'd like to see Satya!" He looked at me, and immediately went inside. He didn't close the door, so I went inside and all the devotees followed. It was a little temple, and the twenty-two people with me sat down and meditated.

I saw some big beautiful marigold flowers and a murti of Mother Kali. A picture of Swamiji's head was in Kali's hand. I was meditating and suddenly I heard someone say loudly, "Get out of here!" When I heard that voice I woke up and saw one of my devotees talking with a foreign man. I got up, took a marigold and a sweet and came outside, and I looked at Swami Satyananda. Right away I recognized him from before. We both looked at each other and both of us were crying. I gave him a little sweet in his mouth and put a marigold flower on his head, and left. No talking, just a brief moment. Then I went back to Calcutta with all the devotees.

She looked me in the eye,
and I knew her immediately.
In the eyes of Shree Maa,
I saw the exact image of Kali,
the deity I had been worshiping for years.
She was incandescent.
So much truth and purity radiated from her face.
I was astonished that the Goddess would come to me.
- Swami Satyananda Saraswati

We came back to Calcutta, and I stayed at Vashishta's house. I knew Swamiji would come, because Mother told me, "Both of you have lots of works to do in this world. He is coming and he will be with you."

For three days I was in samadhi and my devotees were worried I would leave my body soon, because I was in samadhi for so long. Many sadhus said, "If she stays in this state, she will leave her body in a short amount of time." But I wasn't worried, I didn't even know about it.

One day a few weeks later, I was in a very deep samadhi from nine a.m. to the next morning. Three days before I had told Vashishta, "He's coming." That morning, Swamiji knocked on the door and Vashishta opened it and said, "She said you would come!" and Vashishta gave him a big hug! At that time my samadhi broke, and I came downstairs and I looked at Swamiji. Right away Swamiji put his head in my lap, it was so beautiful!

Swamiji didn't talk at that time. He was in samadhi most of the time. I didn't talked with Swamiji because I couldn't understand what he said, and also I hardly ever talked then anyway. Soon after, thousands of people came and it became a different atmosphere.

Swamiji describes meeting Shree Maa as the transformational event in his life.

Swamiji:
From the moment I met her, my life changed. She was purity incarnate, and when I looked into her eyes, I saw divinity made manifest. I never left since that time.

Over the years since I made the commitment to define my life by her presence, I have witnessed so many changes. Yet she remained the same. She is still the 70 pound nuclear reactor that I met that wonderful day in a little village in rural India.

We traveled around India, and she was the same. For me it was both hectic and exciting: a new house every few days, another temple to establish, another puja and yajna to organize, crowds of people that no one could count. Yet she remained the same.

We traveled around America, and she was the same. For me it was amazing: computers everywhere, gadgets you couldn't imagine in everyone's hands, long drives across the wide expanses of American scenery: beaches and mountains, rivers and plains, big cities and small towns; setting up programs in venues around the country, feeding and housing, organizing two dozen devotees who traveled with us. Yet she was the same.

We traveled around Europe, and she was the same. She wrote little songs in the local languages, as we traveled from country to country in the cars and vans. I was harassed by passport and visa formalities, traffic laws, speaking through interpreters, even driving on the wrong side of the road. Yet she remained the same.

We traveled in Africa, Asia, and then around the world, and she was the same. She found something to give to everyone: a song, a cooked meal, a newly sewn cloth, a loving smile, some peace and comfort. I was struggling to communicate, sometimes fearful for our safety, a little bit paranoid. Yet she remained the same.

What is it about that sameness, that equilibrium, balance, poise, grace, which Shree Maa has consistently exhibited throughout her life. She wakes up between three and four AM, no matter what time zone we visit. First she performs japa with the regularity of a time piece. She recites her mantras, counts on her mala of beads. She sits in deep meditation for at least an hour and often several more.

After the completion of her japa and meditation, Shree Maa takes a short walk to the temple and organizes her puja. She worships Lord Shiva every day, but her puja also includes the worship of Ganesh, Durga, Lakshmi, Vishnu, and Saraswati.

After Shree Maa's puja, she performs homa at the sacred fire. Then she gets breakfast, a little cooking and housekeeping, and then she begins her projects. She sews clothing for the devotees, she writes books, edits, approves artwork, records her music, and keeps creatively inspired until past noon; a little lunch, a little rest, and then she sings the Chandi Path.

It is already evening, and Shree Maa prepares the evening meal, talks with devotees around the world, answers correspondence and email, and writes new songs. She is done by 10:00 o'clock, and then she reads scriptures or the lives of saints for an hour or so until she falls asleep.

This is her regular schedule, day in and day out. She only interrupts this rhythm in order to appear in public programs, either through webcasts or with devotees in the temple. But in either case, her bhava remains the same. Shree Maa has a grace and a kindness, a genuine concern for all of her children.

No one can enter her home without being asked, "Have you eaten?" Every ailment, both physical and emotional, is greeted by a patient ear, and more frequently an invaluable solution. She will not hesitate to pick up the phone to contact anyone who may be of help.

And the entire congregation of devotees all around the world understands that Shree Maa is a Divine Mother. Very few could even hope for such a response from their blood related family members. Her being is an example, an inspiration. Her presence is a teaching. She carries herself with such grace, she appears to be of royal lineage. She walks with such humility, the grass bows down before she steps upon it. She requests with such softness and gentility, that anyone would be proud to fulfill her every wish. She commands with such authority, that no one could doubt that following her instructions will result in the highest good.

And that is how my life changed to be in the presence and association with this modern day saint. My faith was renewed; my discipline was inspired; my understanding was increased. With a new vigor I began to study and practice, and search for new ways in which I could share. Her association has made me a better person, and brought me closer to my goals.

MAKING A COMMITMENT TO LIVE

Shree Maa:

After Swami came to see me, we were in Gauhati for a month at Tapash's house. Then I took Swami to Kamakhya to do tapasya and receive Mother Kamakhya's blessing. We did a nine day yagya at the Kamakhya temple with my devotees and then we went back to Tapash's house.

One day I was in samadhi from one in the morning to three or four the next morning. When you go into samadhi, you don't go right away; you get there step by step. At one point it felt like someone was pulling me, like some magnet, was pulling me down in a very strong way.

When I woke up, I saw Swamiji was sitting with his head on my lap. He was sitting on the floor and I was on the bed. The room was full and some devotees were chanting, "Hari Rama, Hari Krishna," and some devotees were meditating deeply, and others were crying. All the devotees knew that if Mother went into samadhi for too long, she might leave her body, so they were reciting mantras to bring me down.

I asked Swamiji, "Why did you bring me back?" and he said, "I want a boon (a wish fulfilling blessing) from you. I said, "What boon do you want?" He said, "I won't tell you until you promise you will give me the boon." When he said that I wasn't completely conscious and I went back into samadhi. After some time, I was feeling very strongly that he was bringing me down again. I came back and asked, "What boon do you want?" He said, "You have to promise me that you will give me the boon." I said, "Yes, I promise you. Tell me now what boon you want." He said, "It's not the time for you to go now; you have to work for this world. Promise you will stay." I said, "Okay, I'll stay and I'll work with you."

People started to cry and it was very beautiful. After that we started to work together. I had forgotten that Kamakhya Maa had previously told me to see Swamiji because I had lots of work in the world to do with him.

THE DIVINE MOTHER APPEARS

One day my worship in the temple came to an end.
I used to worship the Deity in the Kali temple.
It was suddenly revealed to me
that everything is Pure Spirit.
The utensils of worship,
the altar,
the door frame - all Pure Spirit.
Men, animals, and
other living things-all Pure Spirit.
Then like a madman
I began to shower flowers in all directions.
Whatever I saw I worshipped.
-Sri Ramakrishna

There are three modes of perception that are reflected by consciousness: the gross body (using the senses: eyes, ears, nose, skin and tongue), the subtle body (all conceptions) and the causal body (intuition, direct intuitive experience). The clarity and depth of perceptions is therefore subject to the clarity of the reflector, or development of our consciousness, which may be defined as consciousness' ability to operate at up to seven levels simultaneously. Shree Maa's consciousness is operating at all seven levels, her mind totally still, she is able to perceive beyond what others were seeing physically or intellectually or intuitively. She is able to perceive divinity and manifestation of divinity both in the physical forms as well as metaphysical forms. In this chapter Shree Maa shares her experiences with the metaphysical manifestation of divinity.

Again, as a guru, she is teaching us the key message: respect all forms as though they are a manifestation of the Divine Mother. She picks up the story from when Swamiji and some devotee were doing sadhana in the Himalayas and Swamiji got sick.

Shree Maa:

Swamiji became sick, so we took him to a doctor in Assam where he was in treatment for a month. (Laughing) As soon as he got better, he started a nine-day yagya at the Kamakhya temple! There was a big festival celebrating Mother Kamakhya's menstrual period and for three days the temple was closed. Thousands of people were there, and everybody came to see Swamiji's homa.

I was in samadhi while Swamiji was doing the yagya, and one day a dark skinned lady came to the homa. She had curly hair and was chewing betel nut, and red saliva was coming out of her mouth. She put her head in my lap, and she was laughing. My whole cloth became soaked with betel leaves. When I woke up, I saw my whole sari was colored with the red water from her mouth and spotted with oil. She looked at me, and laughed and laughed. She didn't say anything and I didn't say anything. Right away I knew who she was. She was Mother; a form of Mother who came to test. Other people got very upset with her, but it was my way not to say anything.

The next day was the Kamakhya Temple opening, after the third day of her period, and thousands of people were waiting to get into the temple. Our group was standing together when the same lady appeared and all my devotees got upset that she came back. Mahavir asked her, "Where did you come from?" She replied, "You don't know where I live? I live in the cremation grounds. My husband, Pashupati, couldn't come. So I came alone to see you!"

Mahavir was asking questions and she was answering, all the while laughing and laughing. She looked at the people waiting outside the temple and said while laughing, "Look at these people! They want to go inside the temple to bow down, but the real thing is standing here, and nobody comes to bow down!" She was saying this very loudly, "The real thing is here, but nobody is bowing down!" Then she disappeared right in front of all the people. I told Mahavir and the other people, "When you come to the temple, if you see anybody who is acting strangely, or doing something you don't like, never be angry! You don't know who it is!"

When Shankaracharya was alive he was a great pundit and philosopher and a great proponent of nirakara - the formless God. One day he went to take a bath in the Ganges. At that time he had so much pride. When he was coming back from his bath, he saw a dead body, and a woman sitting with the body, crying. Shankaracharya said, "Hey Maa! I have to go. Move that dead body so I can pass!" The mother said, "You are always talking about nirakara, the formless divinity, why don't you move it yourself? You say energy is nothing and form is nothing, then you move it!"

Shankaracharya said, "Are you crazy?" Then that Mother showed Her real form, the form of both Annapurna and Shiva and she said, "You can't talk only about the formless. You have to love energy also - Prakriti. Without Prakriti, there is no Purusha! When Prakriti is doing the divine dance, Purusha is watching - Purusha the infinite consciousness. You can't only talk about Vedanta, you know."

This kind of form you know when Mother appears and disappears; why don't we see that here? In this country there is too much attachment. Mother is coming as a subtle feeling here; she's not coming in form. She is doing subtle work here. Why am I here? That means subtle. She is doing subtle work through me. She will do subtle work through Swamiji, through other people. She is not making Her form here, Herself. She is working with the subtle with everybody. Because She knows in this country, if She takes a form, it would be a big deal. Maybe they would put Her in jail (laughing).

While transcribing this interview, I began to wonder about the subtle ways in which Shree Maa works. I approached a number of people to share their insight with the readers. Gared Price Jones who has been a frequent visitor to the Devi Mandir shares his perception of Shree Maa's ways:

So who is Shree Maa? The question itself is impossible to answer. When I am able to answer it, folks will be asking the same question about me. I suppose the answer to this question - ultimately - is the same as what I'd come to if I ever got to the bottom of the question, "Who am I?"

So... as the pond frog would endeavor to speak of the Amazon, I, too, shall share my puddle's view into Shree Maa and her subtle ways.

In doing so, I am reminded of a parable shared by Sri Ramakrishna about a seeker who was instructed whenever he thought he knew God to think, "Neti-Neti, Not this - Not this." Each glimmer of truth revealed through Shree Maa has simply been a perfect morsel of food, specially prepared for me and especially for that particular moment in time. Her truth is not graspable or meant to be an immutable answer. It is the stuff of impermanence that simply carries one closer to her, to oneself, to bliss, to becoming truth.

So, how subtle are Shree Maa's ways?

She is the sacred journey through the winding hills of Napa. Her presence stretches in time and place well beyond when I actually see her at the Devi Mandir. And, sitting within the temple is like sitting within Shree Maa. I can also sit with her as easily half way around the world.

She offers a universe of generosity and kindness in welcoming me home each visit. Her joy and excitement for me can bring my own tears in a flash. She receives me in the greatest possibility of who I am - far beyond what I trust or believe in myself. And her doing so stretches and affirms my hunger to become just who Shree Maa knows me to be. In her presence I am, in fact, that person!

Shree Maa's way is sacred and blessed in the most simple things in life - the food she prepares, her songs, her prasad, nuts, spices, t-shirts... gifts; especially her smile and laugh and hug. With her, the most basic is the most holy. And, by its nature, it carries its blessing and then passes on.

Shree Maa's presence brings in me clarity and stillness of soul that allows me to truly listen - to her voice and the depths of my own.

As I've had the chance to be a bearer of Shree Maa's wishes and gifts, I've known a cascading of relationships, connections, and unanticipated door-openings that in themselves multiply her blessing (and my own) manifold. Anything touched by Shree Maa is similarly charmed. I have no idea how this works. However, I do know that with Shree Maa it is simply for me to listen and go with whatever comes - in complete trust, faith and joy.

Increasingly I've been finding myself asking, "What can I give to Shree Maa?" Living in the answer to this question, I believe, will be the beginning of my greatest wish coming true.

So, these are a few humble reflections from one lily pad into Shree Maa's Ocean. Never have I met a being who holds (is) the Ocean as Shree Maa. Or one who offers more joy for the diving in.

At the same time I must also bow to her as "Neti-Neti".

PURE DESIRES

In my hallucination I saw my beloved's flower garden.
In my vertigo, in my dizziness, in my drunken haze,
whirling and dancing like a spinning wheel,
I saw myself as the source of existence.
I was there in the beginning
and I was the spirit of love.
Now I am sober.
There is only the hangover
and the memory of love, and the sorrow.
I yearn for happiness, I ask for help, I want mercy,
and my Love says: Look at me and hear me
because I am here just for that.
-Rumi

Even great sufi poet Rumi yearned for happiness. The existence of every individual soul is bound by desires. Were there no desires, there would be no individuality. However, the pure desires will take us to the state of desirelessness. The impure desires will bind us more securely and take us deeper into the field of isolation and loneliness. Both desires will create bondage; however, by surrendering the object of desire, we can free ourselves from bondage. In the following stories we will learn how Shree Maa is bound by pure desires and how by surrendering the object of her desires, she frees herself from bondage.

In the last talk, Shree Maa told how Swamiji had asked for the boon that she stay in her body. After that Shree Maa traveled with Swamiji and some devotees. She picks up the story when they arrived in the mountain town of Rishikesh.

Shree Maa:

We went to Rishikesh with Vashishta and other devotees. For three months we did sadhana from morning to evening. Swamiji, Vashishta, and the other devotees weren't eating anything until evening, when I cooked a little kitcheree.

I was cooking kitcheree with a few vegetables at about six o'clock one evening, when I went into samadhi. My meditation broke about two in the morning, and when I woke up I saw everybody was sleeping. I thought, "What? Is it day or night?" I looked at a watch and saw it was two a.m. Then I looked at the stove and saw that they hadn't eaten the food, because I hadn't served them. I was so sad and I said to my self, "These children didn't eat because I didn't serve them. What did I do?"

After that, I was talking (intuitive conversation) with Jesus. Then I looked at Swamiji, and thought, "If you are really doing His work, and you are that, then wake up! If you're doing His karma, and the same activities, and you came to purify this world, you wake up!" Swamiji had a blanket covering his face, and he peeked out and opened the blanket and started laughing. I started to cry loudly! It made me cry because I got my answer right away!

Then everyone else woke up and asked, "What happened?" I said, "You could have eaten by yourselves, but you are so devoted that you wouldn't eat without taking it from my hand. Seeing your devotion made me cry." Then I fed all of them.

After that, we went to the Himalayas, where we took a three month sankalpa. After some time we ended up at Upper Jageshvara where lots of miracles happened. In one spot we celebrated Navaratri and we wanted to share prasad with the people nearby when the festival was over. There were very few people in the

village, so I made only forty ladhus (a sweet, shaped round like a ball). When Navaratri was complete, hundreds of children came as if from nowhere, and I gave to each a ladhu. They came back every day, and everyone still got a ladhu. We fed all those children for three days with those forty ladhus and there were still some left over.

Jageshwar in the Himalayas

DANCING MONKEYS

One day I was near the Ganges and I was in samadhi. When I woke up, I suddenly had a strong desire to see monkeys. I don't know why I wanted to see them. I went into a nearby temple and asked the priest, "Have you seen any monkeys here?" The priest said, "Mother, it's very rare to see monkeys here. There were lots of monkeys here a long time ago, but now you're lucky to see one or two."

The next day I came to the same spot and went into samadhi. When I woke up there were hundreds of monkeys covering the trees nearby and the whole mountain. They were dancing and eating leaves and making lots of noise! They had an ash color. The whole village came out to see, and I sang a song to Rama and the monkeys started dancing! Swamiji came out and offered them prasad.

You know, the really great things in my life are presents from God. Whatever desires I have, God always fulfills them. Sometimes a desire will come to me that I'd like to eat a samosa, but there are no samosas around. Then in the morning, I would see a big samosa package on the table! God always fulfills pure desires.

When we are One with God, whatever one wants, God always gives it to the person. But when a desire has attachment, it's hard to get fulfilled. When a desire has attachment, there is trouble. A pure desire is always fulfilled.

VASHISHTA'S UMBRELLA

We were in Upper Jageshwara at the top of the mountain, where we did a fifteen-day sankalpa. In Upper Jageshwara you can't get any food, there is nothing around, so you have to go several miles to get anything. If you leave at six in the morning, you will reach the nearest place in the midday and return in the late afternoon.

One day, I took one of my devotees, Ratan, with me to town. We left at six in the morning. He wanted to take Vashishta's umbrella because sometimes it rained. I told him, "Don't take that umbrella. If we get wet, we get wet." Vashishta didn't like to lend his umbrella because it once belonged to Swami Brahmananda, one of Ramakrishna's

148

direct disciples. After that it was given to Swami Abhutananda. A disciple gave it to Vashishta, because he was such a great man, and he always kept that umbrella with him. But Ratan didn't listen to me and he secretly took it with us.

At midday, I don't care where I am, I have to take a shower and sit down to pray! In India, I didn't care where I was; I took a shower anywhere. While I was praying, Ratan took the umbrella and went to another part of the bazaar.

When he came back I said (Laughing), "Where is the umbrella?"

He said, "Oh, Ram, Ram, Ram!" He ran back to all the stores he had visited looking for the umbrella, but he couldn't find it. He said, "Ah, what will happen to me?"

Vashishta didn't want to lend it, and Ratan took it without Vashishta's permission, and Ratan didn't listen to me, and now he lost it.

We got back to the temple at about seven at night and Vashishta asked, "Mother, where is my umbrella?" I said, "Oh, I gave it away to somebody." He said, "I don't believe it. You gave it away, Mother?" I said, "Yes, I gave it away. You came to the Himalayas to do tapasya, why are you attached to this umbrella? You have to think about God! Why are you thinking about your umbrella? You don't think I gave it away?" He said, "No, I don't think you gave it away."

I didn't say anymore. The second day, he said, "Mother, did you really give away my umbrella?" I said, "Yes, don't you believe me? Yes, I gave it away." He was quiet.

The third day he said, "Mother, I don't believe you when you say you gave my umbrella away. What did you do?" (Laughing) I was so upset! I said, "Again, you are talking about the umbrella. I don't want to listen anymore. Never talk about that umbrella again!"

Right away, I went to the temple where there was a big Shiva lingam. (Laughing) I pointed at Shiva and told Him, "Again he is talking about the umbrella. This is your fault! Find out about that umbrella!"

The Shiva Lingam where Shree Maa worshiped

Within two days our sankalpa was finished and we were ready to go. Then a big storm came and the rain was unbelievable. When the bus came, we got on and I sat down near a closed window. Then we came to the town and a little boy ran up to the bus yelling, "Mataji! Mataji!" He started banging on the window as the bus drove through the bazaar and he was yelling, "Mataji, Mataji, your umbrella, your umbrella!" Swamiji yelled, "Driver, please stop the bus!"

The little boy came aboard the bus and found me and said, "Mataji, this is your umbrella." I threw that umbrella to Vashishta saying, "Take your umbrella!" (Laughing) And Vashishta cried and cried. Nobody could stop his crying. Isn't that beautiful? Look, I told Shiva, and Shiva came as a little boy and gave me that umbrella to keep Vashishta's faith. Unbelievable! Now I think it's unbelievable, but at that time I never thought that.

Ramya Srinivasan and Srinivasan Rangan, both professors at University of Colorado who, a few years ago, left brilliant academic careers to pursue a path of spirituality, share their experiences with Shree Maa as follows:

We received an email notice in our university saying "A Bengali saint is to visit our campus in a Hinduism class." A small group of us were excited that a saint would come to campus and went to see Her! The talk was held in a large size auditorium. Swamiji gave an amazingly inspiring talk, while Maa was sitting beside Him in silent meditation. At the end of the talk, several students and people in the audience asked questions. Swamiji answered each and every question with His characteristic enthusiasm and divine wisdom. We all sat spell bound just watching and listening to Him. An Indian man sitting in the middle of the room asked, "Whatever we may do, I have heard that without Guru's grace nothing is possible." So saying the man started sobbing. Suddenly, Shree Maa arose and ever so gently and gracefully walked up to the man and hugged him and said, "Stay like this, you will get." Her words, Her grace, Her beauty were so powerful and yet so simple and humble that it is impossible to describe that moment in mere words.

The first thing that we noticed when in Shree Maa's presence was Her aura of stillness and peace. She is continually in a state of stillness and moves in a state of stillness. And when we are in Her presence, the power of that pure stillness fills us, and our thoughts are transformed. From the mental space of worldliness and activity, we find ourselves in the space of pure peace. Once we taste this peace, we begin to wonder about its source. We long for it; our minds hanker for it. And the journey with Shree Maa begins.

If anybody spends even a few seconds in Shree Maa's presence, they can feel Her peace, pure love for all existence and simple joy. Maa's every moment is filled with divinity. Her lips speak about God and every action She offers to God. Her thoughts are pure and free from any taint of selfishness. She is the highest and a most beautiful ideal of perfection in a human life. Shree Maa encourages us and teaches all of us to strive to such a pure ideal and mold our lives for God. Maa takes every opportunity to teach us also to strive for purity and truth and make our lives an offering to God.

Shree Maa speaks very little, yet when she does, Her words combine beauty, simplicity, and profound wisdom that transforms. Once, when I was in Her presence, Shree Maa offered me (Rangan) a glass of juice. I accepted the glass and drank the juice. I then washed the glass and set it on the dish stand without drying the glass or putting it away. Immediately, Shree Maa said, "Complete your karma, dry the glass and put it away." She added, "If you do not complete your karma in this life, you will have to be born again; and you do not want to come back again to suffer in this world." This simple teaching had an immediate and powerful effect on me. I reflect on it from time to time; and I never fail to dry and put away the dishes that I eat or drink from!

She said to me once, "When you do seva for your husband, think of your ishta devata (beloved deity). Think you are doing seva to Shiva or Narayana or any form of God you love." She said that this should be my attitude while cooking in the kitchen and doing seva to any of my brothers and sisters - always think you are serving God. A few weeks after getting this advice from Shree Maa, I had to teach an executive management class to a group of 40 managers. I was very nervous as the class was composed of all middle-aged men. My husband gently advised me, "Why do you worry? Remember Shree Maa's advice. Just think they are all forms of Gopal. What a glorious chance you have - to play with 40 Gopals!" Somewhat reassured, I went into the classroom. I gave an overview of the syllabus and announced that I would like the class to be interactive with participation from all the students and we should all know each other's names. Suddenly, one man in the middle of the class raised his hand and said, "My name is Gopal!" I had to laugh at Gopal's tricks and Shree Maa's sweet advice!

We were a small group sitting in the temple after arati. Shree Maa turned to me and said, "If you think of your mother as your mother, you will create karma. If you think of her as Divine Mother, you will be free." As I was pondering this, Shree Maa went on to explain that we can see all people as a form of God based on their actions. For example, you see somebody creating something new, you can think of Lord Brahma. You see somebody taking care of everything; you can see Lord Vishnu in them. Sometimes you see someone giving knowledge; they are a form of Lord Shiva. Shree Maa said that when She walked into the temple in the morning, She looked at the carpet and saw the beautiful design and thought of Goddess Saraswati. She said that when we went out She did not look at people, but saw them as forms of God and Goddess. This lesson had such a profound effect on all of us. It was so simple, powerful and beautiful. For weeks after that, we were referring to each other as forms of deities and feeling love and respect in our interactions.

One time we were cleaning a room to prepare it for guests. All of us were cleaning the counter tops vigorously to make sure they were spotless. Everything was put away and clean, clean, clean was the mantra on our lips.

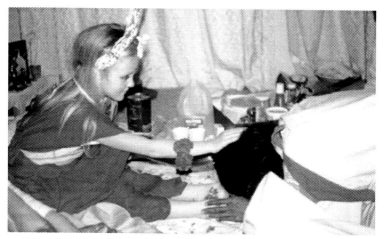

Shree Maa bowing at the feet of a young girl as a living Goddess

When we were done, Shree Maa came and smiled, "Okay, now make beauty." In less than a minute, She took some flowers from a vase nearby and cut them and arranged them in smaller vases and decorated with candles and laid everything out artistically. Shree Maa taught us, "Satyam, Shivam, Sundaram - Truth, Consciousness, Beauty." If you live in truth with beauty, you will get pure consciousness.

Once we were arranging an altar in the temple and Shree Maa said, "Make beauty. Then God will come." Be it in the kitchen, the guest rooms, the temple, wherever Shree Maa goes, She makes beauty - Her very touch creates joy and beauty. She teaches us to enjoy the process of making everything clean and beautiful - ready to receive the highest guest always - God.

Shree Maa has no personal agenda. She only wants us to be divine. Her mission is to purify our hearts so that we can see God inside. And as She strives to purify us, She demonstrates untiring patience. Even as we repeatedly fall, making the same mistakes, as our loving Mother, Maa picks us up, brushes us off, and points us forward. Shree Maa often says, "Never look back, always move forward."

Once I was walking by Shree Maa's side, I was overwhelmed by her beauty and grace and stammered, "Maa, I love you." Shree Maa chose to ignore that remark. We continued walking into her house where She opened a cabinet and gave me some medicine (I had a cold) and lovingly explained how often I should take it.

Shree Maa is famous, and yet humble. Only true lovers of God can live with fame and yet remain unaffected by it. Shree Maa has thousands of devotees around the world. People long to have Her darshan, and are constantly calling Her seeking Her advice and love. She is widely acknowledged as the highest example of peace and devotion. Yet Shree Maa lives as a simple child of God. She carries Herself as if She does not exist. She is the living Goddess, yet She worships the Divine Mother and Father with the greatest devotion that can be conceived. She is the Guru, yet She will not lose an opportunity to serve Her own disciples. Her wisdom is infinite, yet Her language has no "big talk" in it, only pure love.

The nature of the mind is desire. Constantly thoughts come and they become desires that are colored by selfishness. Shree Maa often tells me that even if there is a small amount of selfishness in our hearts, we cannot attain the highest state, become one with God. Shree Maa's own life is a demonstration of continuous selflessness. She gives over and over again, indiscriminately. Whether she is comforting her children around the world with Her wisdom and love, making gifts and food for all who walk into Her bandhar, or praying for suffering humanity around the world, Shree Maa has no thought for Herself. Why else would She accept such an unworthy soul as myself in Her holy abode? Why would She feed me and love me? And constantly guide me to God?

Shree Maa answers our most sincere call without fail. If we pray to Her with a full heart, She will hear us wherever we are in the world. Once I was in India and was chanting the scripture Chandi Path in my family's prayer room. When I came to the verse where we ask the Goddess for a boon, I became overcome with emotion and prayed that I could serve Shree Maa in some way. After completing the recitation, I forgot about this request and went to check my email. I had an email from Swamiji. Swamiji said that Shree Maa wanted me to do something for Her!

Shree Maa is Shiva, She is Sri Ramakrishna, She is a Divine Goddess. Why tarry? Hold on to Her and She will take you across this ocean of Samsara! She is Satyam, Shivam, Sundaram: truth, the consciousness of infinite goodness, and beauty. Glory to our most beloved mother, Shree Maa! Victory to She who eternally lives in Satya Yuga! May we be inspired to follow Her holy example and make our lives a holy offering to God.

PURE LOVE NEVER CHANGES

We bloomed in Spring.
Our bodies are the leaves of God.
The apparent seasons of life and death our eyes can suffer;
but our souls, dear, I will just say this forthright:
they are God Himself,
we will never perish until He does.
-Saint Teresa of Avila

Shree Maa continued with her story about the period when she and Swamiji first began teaching together.

Shree Maa:

Swamiji was staying at Vashishta's house with me and lots of devotees came to see him. It was very interesting, because many people came from Bombay, Delhi, West Bengal and other places. They saw Jesus in their dreams telling them, "Come and see me." Jesus even said where he was, and that was where Swamiji was staying. All these people came to see Swamiji.

When people love Truth, and people love pure love, they have a connection with all higher souls. When a higher soul comes, they will find them. They loved Jesus, they saw him in their dreams, and they came to see him. They were really pure devotees.

The President of the West Bengal Education Department came to see him, and started crying and held Swamiji to his shoulder like he was holding a little baby. Hundreds of people were crying along with him. It was such a wonderful bhava; it was an unbelievable moment! This feeling was happening day after day, it was beautiful.

It was an incredible time! It felt like everything was heaven! There was no doubt, there was just pure devotion, we were swimming in devotion. Those first couple of years when Swamiji came, it was unbelievable!

When I was young, Jesus told me that he couldn't finish his study in India in that lifetime. He was very involved with the Vedas and Sanskrit, but he could not finish learning them. He told me that he would come in another form and complete that work. He could not finish this work, so another body would come and finish that karma.

In that way Swamiji came. Isn't that beautiful how the soul works - body to body, body to body. Do you understand? I think that whoever has knowledge will understand this. If I say, "Jesus told me he is coming in another body to finish his karma," nowadays people wouldn't believe it, because of their lack of knowledge; but the soul always works this way.

For example, at the time when Shankaracharya was alive he defeated all the pundits in India. There was also another great pundit in India who nobody could defeat. Shankaracharya went there to debate, and the pundit's wife got upset, thinking, "My husband has never been beaten, and now Shankaracharya will defeat him!"

Shankaracharya said to the pundit, "If I defeat you, you'll be my disciple. If you defeat me, I'll be your disciple." Ultimately, Shankaracharya defeated him. Suddenly his wife, who was also a great debater, appeared and said, "You don't know everything! You don't know kama sutra, you don't know married life. Explain the meaning of the kama sutra to me." Shankaracharya couldn't give an answer because he had been a brahmachari (celibate) his whole life. He told her, "Give me a month, then I'll give you an answer."

At that time, a king in one state died. Shankaracharya knew that the king had left his body and he told his disciple, "Watch my body, I'm going to the king's body to do some work." The disciple protected Shankaracharya's body in a cave, while Shankaracharya went to the king's body and the king became alive again.

Now that king had been a very bad king and when Shankaracharya entered his body, he became a good king. His wife thought, "This isn't my husband, he's too good." After one month, Shankaracharya came back to his original body, and then he returned to answer the pundit's wife's questions about the kama sutra.

What Jesus told me was, "I am coming back, and I will finish all the karma." Isn't that beautiful? Every human does the same thing, but we live in so much darkness, we don't know ourselves. If you compare Swamiji to Jesus, people won't understand because nowadays people live completely in the dark. They don't know about the soul, they don't know about karma. They will start to fight, because they can't see.

For that purpose, Swamiji came back to me. So many people saw these dreams and the dreams came alive! Hundreds of people were crying. You wouldn't believe that moment!

SWAMIJI'S EXPLANATION

There is a possibility that a reader might misinterpret Shree Maa's comments about Jesus in this chapter, so I asked Swamiji to add a few words of clarification. The following is his explanation.

Swamiji:

I think when Indians equated me with Jesus; it was more a case of racial profiling, like when people in this country thought that Sikhs wearing turbans were members of Al Qaeda.

The only white people Indians knew, the Britishers, were seen as very stern and formal, and held the Indian culture in complete disdain.

The only other white man to which Indians had been exposed was Jesus Christ, who is considered to be a great saint throughout India. There is a picture of him in many homes, often in association with Ramakrishna, especially where there is a large concentration of Christians. So the Indians had seen many pictures of a white man with long hair and a beard, wearing robes and dedicating himself to spiritual life as a sadhu.

When these Indians saw me, they saw a long-haired, white, bare feet, broke sadhu, devoting his life to God and Sanskrit. They tried to create a profile for me and thought,

"He's obviously not a Britisher and he speaks our language. What other example do we have from the Western tradition but the story of Christ?"

My ability to chant Sanskrit created another association with Jesus. What white man knew Sanskrit? There was only the popular story of Jesus studying Sanskrit in Benares. So that's how the association with Jesus came about. I wasn't chanting in Latin, or teaching Christianity, or even talking about Christ.

Now here was Shree Maa, who was a recognized, validated saint with a tremendous following, and here was this Western sadhu who did pujas and chanted the Chandi, who people associated with Jesus.

Soon the word got out that Jesus was staying with Shree Maa in Calcutta. The news traveled so fast from this region to that region, from Calcutta to Bombay that soon the whole neighborhood filled up. You couldn't walk in the lanes towards the houses where we stayed. Thousands of people congregated without the benefit of advertising, newspapers, or television. The energy was effervescent and kept growing and growing.

When people heard that Jesus was in Calcutta with Shree Maa, they would wake up and say, "I just dreamed of Jesus and I'm going to Calcutta!" Now it is also true that some people dreamed about Jesus being in Calcutta, who hadn't heard about us at all.

Many people came and made offerings, but we didn't want it, and we didn't need it. They put money at our feet and we would just walk away. They

160

gave Shree Maa saris and she would give them to the poor. I would said, "Maa, can't you save just one for yourself?" and she would reply, "When I will need a sari, it will come."

THE SAME KARMA

When Shree Maa says I have the same karma as Jesus, she means that, like Jesus, I am trying to inspire people to love God. I have the same agenda as Jesus did: to love God with all my heart and all my soul and all my might, and to love my neighbor as my self.

Another similarity in our karma is that we have the same determination and capacity to cross over the divide that separates the West from the East, the white people from the brown people.

Jesus was a student of Sanskrit grammar and philosophy in India. But because he was perceived as a threat to the Brahmins, he wasn't able to complete his sadhana in Sanskrit. Therefore that same bhava (spiritual feeling) had to come in a different body to complete this sadhana.

The individual who came to complete Jesus's work had to possess the ability to transcend discrimination. He had to be able to cross over all boundaries so he could enter into the mystery, the hidden part of Sanskrit. He also had to be able to decipher Sanskrit into a romance language so Westerners could understand both Sanskrit and the Indian culture it came from. He needed to be able to translate the subtle experiences, and describe the practices by which these experiences could be internalized.

This is a very specific mission that Jesus was not able to complete in his lifetime. So someone had to come back and complete it.

WE ARE ALL COMPLETING HIS KARMA

Even if one person in the West gets illuminated with bhava, gets ignited with the fire of devotion, with true sincerity and determination, then Jesus's quest for sharing this knowledge from the East will have been fulfilled.

We need to create an understanding among the people of the world that all wisdom is coming from the same place. If we can move away from external forms into the inner experience, we will all reach the same perspective. Then we will unite and stop all the fighting and division.

This is the unfinished business of all humanity. Jesus is the embodiment of all pervading love in the world. My body came back to help fulfill that unfinished aspiration of all humanity. So did everybody else's. Some of us wake up to this calling sooner, some of us wake up to it later. We're all here to create universal harmony. We're all here to manifest the Christ as the embodiment of universal love, we're all here to tear down the barriers and experience the unity of all existence.

If you're here to serve others, then come on; let's go to work. You're on the same team with Jesus, Ramakrishna, Mohammed, Moses and all the other heavy hitters. You're a slugger, you're on the team; you're chosen. God wants you!

SHREE MAA BECOMES DANGEROUS

For Shree Maa, being a sadhu is being divine, speaking of divinity and inspiring divinity in others. There are a number of stories where she has confronted sadhus who are not living up to the standard, or who are just frauds.

Here is one such story from Shree Maa:

Remember when I talked about a doctor who was paralyzed? He saw a dream about Jesus too, and I decided I should go to his house and stay there with Swamiji. We did a big Durga Puja there in Gauhati and the whole city knew a foreign sadhu was doing Durga Puja and a nine days fire ceremony. It was unbelievable that a foreign sadhu could do this. People fell in love with him! Nobody wanted to leave Swamiji.

In the same way as in the life of Jesus, when Swamiji started to talk about truth and pure love, a couple of sadhus got jealous. When we came back to Calcutta, some sadhus started to say bad things about him and me.

Many devotees were coming to me and saying, "Mother! This sadhu is saying this, this sadhu is saying that." And I said, "Ok, just listen." One day I got so mad! I asked, "Where is that sadhu staying?" I told everybody, "Hey! Tomorrow at three a.m., everybody come with me, and we will go to see that sadhu." At three o'clock we started to walk, there was no bus or car, and we reached the sadhu's house at six o'clock. I told the sadhu, "All these children are talking about these things that you are saying. Is it true?" He didn't give an answer.

There were more than twenty devotees with me. I asked one of them, "Now say what this sadhu said!" I asked each person this question and one by one, they answered. I said to the sadhu, "For this purpose you came to do dharma in this world? You are a sadhu, and you are doing this karma? Please, make everything divine." Then we left and after that, there was no more talking. I didn't hear anything and I don't think he said anything.

Yeah, I was dangerous.

BANGLADESH SECTARIAN VIOLENCE

Keep knocking,
and the joy inside will
eventually open a window
and look out
to see who is there.
- Rumi

Shree Maa picked up the narrative after the appearance and disappearance of the Mother at the Kamakhya temple in Assam.

Shree Maa:
In 1980, we did Durga Puja two times. The Durga Puja at Belur Math was Swamiji's first time performing a puja publicly. A rumor had spread that a foreign sadhu was doing Durga Puja and thousands of people came to see. We made a statue of Ramakrishna and another of Mahishasura Mardhini with her eighteen hands. People came from all over - Bangladesh, Assam, Delhi, Bombay, Rishikesh, and Calcutta.

Many swamis came to see why we made a Ramakrishna statue, and why a foreign sadhu was performing a puja. Some swamis were very happy and some swamis were not so happy because they feared a challenge to their monastic order.

It became a beautiful celebration. Swamiji brought everybody to life! He was teaching about puja and worship and every moment he was giving knowledge! He was saying, "Wake up!" People had never felt so much inspiration at a Mother puja before. It was an incredible time.

After that Durga Puja, we came back to Calcutta, and we went with a few devotees to Bangladesh for three months. Bangladesh is a Muslim country, and when we got down from the bus at the station, we saw that the people there were so afraid! Swamiji went to get the tickets for the bus, and many people surrounded me, saying, "Who are you? What are you doing here?" When I said I came from Kamakhya, everybody got scared, words started to buzz, and it became even more crowded. People were telling each other, "This lady came from Kamakhya!"

Everybody knew that Kamakhya was a very powerful place. If a person isn't pure, he becomes afraid. They thought Kamakhya was a tantric place where one can do anything, good or bad.

Swamiji came back, and we got on a bus. We had a trunk with us where Swamiji kept all his puja things. One boy started to talk with Swamiji, asking where he came from, and so on. He wanted to stay with us. I was sitting at another place on the bus and when I meditated, I saw the boy was a gunda, a thief. I said to that boy, "Do you know where we're going? We're going to the District Magistrate's (Chief of Police's) house. If you go with us, you'll get caught." At the next stop, he got off.

We stayed at the District Magistrate's house for three months. We also traveled all over Bangladesh doing worship and puja. Then Shiva Ratri (one of the holiest nights for Hindus which is dedicated to Shiva) came and forty-five Hindus were celebrating with us. Suddenly, more than a hundred Muslim men came with pitchforks and spears. They were standing below, because we were on a little bit elevated platform. I was in samadhi and just then my body started to burn and I had to come back.

When I opened my eyes, I saw the Muslim people standing with the weapons. Swamiji ran and sat down in front of me. But I got up and sat down in front of the Muslims, who were still standing. I said, "Why are you doing this? Does it bother you if we pray to God?" No one

Shree Maa gives blessings

answered. I said, "Why are you trying to start a fight? Aren't we all human beings? Don't you have any love? You do your karma, they do their karma, what is the reason for fighting? If our chanting is disturbing you, should we stop calling to God!" They still didn't answer.

Then I said, "If you want to kill someone, kill me! First kill me, and then do whatever you want." Everyone was quiet. They didn't say one word, and then they left. So we finished our yajna. You can see how angry they were.

On the second night, we went to another village and did a homa. A rich Hindu businessman came to the homa that night. When he was returning home by boat, he was killed!

166

Shree Maa and Swamiji performing homa at a village

Every night we had satsangha and Swamiji and I talked about the Devi Bhagavatam. One Muslim boy, about twenty-seven years old, came every night, from midnight to two a.m. He listened to Swamiji's wisdom and said, "If they knew I was coming to a Hindu house to listen to Hindu philosophy, they would kill me. Why are we fighting with each other? I don't understand. I'm sorry I was born into a Muslim family."

We made that house into a beautiful temple. On one side was Ramakrishna, in the middle was Jesus, on the other side Mecca. Every night we would have satsangha. This news spread, mouth to mouth - from Muslim spiritual leaders to other Muslim spiritual leaders. They said to each other, "A foreign sadhu has come, and he is following Hindu culture, and they have an altar for Mecca, Jesus and Ramakrishna."

I knew there would be danger one night. I was in samadhi from five to eleven o'clock and so many Muslim people came that night. The whole room was packed! There were a hundred spiritual leaders from all over Bangladesh. This was the first time Muslims had been allowed inside the Hindu Magistrate's house.

They wanted to know why we made an altar with Mecca next to a Hindu shrine and a Christian shrine.

I came out of samadhi and suddenly, a Muslim name came out of my mouth. I said to that person, "Can you give me a glass of pani? I'd like a drink." Pani is the word for water in the Muslim language. He was surprised and wondered, "How does Mother know my name?" He was shaking and thinking, "Will Mother drink water from my hand?" They gave him a big brass cup and he brought it to me and I drank from his hand.

After that I said to a Hindu boy, "Babalu, give me a glass of jal." Jal is water in the Bengali language. I drank that water also. After that, I said to Swamiji, "Swami, please give me a glass of water." Swamiji brought a glass of water and I drank it.

I said to all the Muslims, "Look! This water isn't doing anything to me! I drank from a Muslim's hand, I drank from a white man's hand, I drank from a Hindu's hand. It's the same water. We are also the same. Why are you fighting? Why are you trying to find out if this person is a Christian, that person is a Hindu, or that person is a Muslim, or another is a Buddhist? Keep the dharma of love and share that love with everybody and there will be peace. We are all children of God."

A couple of the Muslim leaders knelt down and cried. Everybody felt that we were one and everyone felt good. They said, "You have to go from village to village and give this knowledge, we need this knowledge in our country." They prayed with us and left.

THE CHILLUM SADHU

A big rumor started all over Bangladesh that a couple of Hindu sadhus were here, and people started to come. At that time, I was always in samadhi. One day while I was in samadhi, I felt something was not right, some impurity was burning my body. When I woke up, a woman said, "Maa? There is a sadhu here. Swamiji is in samadhi, and that sadhu is with Swamiji face to face, and he's trying to defeat Swamiji in a defiant way." The sadhu knew a little tantra vidya, negative action, and was trying to fight with Swamiji by disrupting his meditation by his mantras. That's what was bothering me. Right away I went to the house where Swamiji was and I saw he was in samadhi, and this sadhu was trying to do things to him.

When I got there, the sadhu started to shake. He stopped everything, and looked at me. Then I brought Swamiji back with me to the house where I was staying. I put Swamiji in the other room. Swamiji was only drinking juice then, so we gave him some coconut juice.

Then the sadhu came to the house I had brought Swamiji to. We had made a fire place inside the house and he sat in front of it and started smoking a big chillum of ganja (marijuana). Somebody came to me and said, "Mother! That sadhu is smoking."

I got so mad! I came to him and said, "You are wearing orange (the color of renunciation), and this is the kind of education you are giving?" He didn't reply. I said, "I'm going to beat you!" I took his chillum from his mouth, and I put it in the middle of the howan kund while the fire was going. I said, "If you're brave, take that chillum out of this fire! If you really want God, I'd like to see you take back that chillum!"

He didn't take it. He said, "I want a promise from you!"
I said, "Yessss... What promise do you want?" He said, "If I
am giving up my chillum, then I want to live with you." I
said, "You can live with me on the subtle plane. Do strong
sadhana, and you will get the Mother in a subtle way! But
don't just wear that orange dress to show people you're a
sadhu, you have to do sadhana!"

WE ARE ONE FAMILY

Some Muslim men took us to many different places to
meet their scholars. A Muslim professor of English had a
big library with books about Vedantic, Hindu, Christian,
Buddhist and Muslim philosophy. He said to Swamiji, "I
don't understand Hindu philosophy. They make statues;
they do puja. I don't understand these things." He was also
a spiritual leader. He said in a very rough way, "Why is
Kali sticking out her tongue? Why is She standing on
Shiva? These things don't make sense."

Swamiji was calm and quiet, and he explained that
Kali's tongue was red because She is drinking all our
desires. She is black because She is taking all of our
darkness. She is standing on Shiva because Shiva is
watching Her infinite dance (all drama in the Universe),
and He is completely in bliss.

The Muslim professor said, "I've never heard this kind
of explanation before!" He asked lots of questions, and he
was so pleased with Swamiji. He said, "We need you! Stay
here a couple of years and give lectures. I think you will
bring peace to this part of the world."

After that, lots of leaders came to see Swamiji to ask
questions, it was so beautiful.

The next year, we did Durga Puja at Calcutta again.
People were surprised to see this foreign sadhu talking

about the Vedas and performing different kinds of worship. He made people realize that we are one family. The feeling was unbelievable, unspeakable. Every day was a whole new creation.

They'd probably never seen anybody like Swamiji. No, never.

BAMANGACHI

A devotee named Tewariji was living in a town called Bamangachi where someone was being killed every day because of political unrest. Tewariji said, "Mataji, please perform Durga Puja here to cure this place." I said, "Yes, I would love to do that." Other people said, "That's impossible! Every day there are people throwing bombs and fighting and dying."

Swamiji called all the opposing political party leaders together. The Calcutta police were always looking for these guys. Somehow, we got those parties of political people

together to talk and Swamiji said, "We would like to do Durga Puja here, if you would protect us."

They all said, "We would like to do that." They weren't gundas; they were a political party, two parties against each other; killing each other every night. You wouldn't believe it. I was living on the third floor and every night bomb, bomb and bomb!

We did a nine day Durga Puja and it was so beautiful! A couple of hundred people were fasting for nine days. We made an immense howan kund to accommodate a lot of people and built a fence around it. We didn't allow all the people to make an offering into the fire, only those who were fasting. Two hundred people were fasting, and they were doing homa for twenty-four hours. It was so beautiful, so beautiful. Everyone was wearing white clothes. All the girls that were fasting were wearing red-bordered saris. At night, all the political people kept quiet. They didn't fight at all, but stood guard to protect our puja.

For nine days I was in samadhi for much of the time. On the last day, I was feeling, "Today all the girls will do arati with lotus flowers." I didn't tell anyone. Then, all the girls came to me and said, "Mother, today all the women would like to do arati."

Swamiji was doing a big fire! Purnima saw Mother Chamunda coming from the fire. She saw the form of Chamunda Kali and she fainted. No one knew why she fainted, and later she told us, "Chamunda Maa came!" She was unconscious for a couple of hours. So beautiful!

And a snake came. The snake went around the howan kund three times. That night, all women danced beautifully and men who couldn't see them, jumped over the barrier and they started dancing too. Everyone was giving Swamiji garlands. He was completely covered with garlands (Laughing).

After that, peace came. It was completely peaceful. I can't tell you those couple of years were incredible. After that puja we had to leave, we had to hide, so we went to Rishikesh because too many people knew us. It was becoming really crowded.

You know a message comes from everything - from both bad and good events. For example, America has been attacked. (This interview was seven months after 9-11). What message are we getting? Aren't we getting the message to wake up? And everyone is feeling a need to pray to God; the feeling, "Oh God!" (Laughing)

How beautiful! How ignorant we are sometimes. We forget ourselves. But actually every moment we can learn from everybody. We are human beings, we can be beautiful and have beautiful lives.

And yet people forget so quickly. Once that crisis fades a little bit, most people slip right back into their old ways of doing things. Why do they forget? Because they don't do tapasya. Why do we call this time of the Kali Yuga, the "Dark Age?" Because everyone is too busy to remember God.

You know, in olden times, in the Vedic times, everyone was remembering God. It was very peaceful and God was felt everywhere. Then the population gradually increased and people got busier and began to forget. People don't think, "OK, we have enough material possessions, now we should turn to God." Instead they say, "I want more! I want name, fame, gain!" (Laughing) Fun! Isn't that fun?

These days the world is tough and the mind is pulling us everywhere. When the mind pulls, you become a wave (she makes up and down waving motion with hands). Therefore, the Chandi is the best book for our times. When Markandeya wrote the Chandi, he knew this time in the world was coming. Before destruction comes, it will be dark. He knew human beings would forget the dharma. Therefore he wrote the Chandi to deal with these fluctuations of the mind. In every chapter he wrote how the asuras (forces of confusion) are affecting us. He wrote the Chandi so that when people read it, it will remind them who they are so they can cut the ego. Isn't it beautiful? He wrote to protect human beings and to tell them that "I am with you, I am that." Ultimately it will become "I am that."

GOING TO AMERICA

I'm not giving you up
No matter how you glare at me.
What's all this teasing and tricks, Mother,
When I go to get what's mine?
I've got Shiva's promissory note Signed and sealed in my heart.
Now I'm going to take you to His court
And get a ruling.
I'll show what kind of son you've got when the hearing begins.
I've also got the deed of my guru to show the court.
This trial between us is going to be a beauty, Mother.
And I'm not going to settle until you take me lovingly to You.
-Ramprasad Sen

In this last interview, Shree Maa brings her story to a close by describing how and why she and Swamiji came to the United States.

SWAMIJI ON FIRE

Shree Maa:

In 1983 we were performing austerities with some devotees in the Himalayas for three months. I told everybody that in eight days, something would happen to Swamiji. I asked them all to watch out for him because I would be in samadhi much of the time.

On the eighth day I was in samadhi, and I felt that my body was burning. It became very hot. I woke up and came back to my own consciousness. When I opened my eyes, I saw Swamiji was on fire! His cloth was burning. One whole side of the howan kund had been stacked with wood to dry, and that wood was also burning! He was still saying, "Swaha, swaha, I am one with God, I am one with God!" He was chanting the Chandi, and he didn't care if his body was burning completely! His lunghi (a cloth for the lower body) was on fire. I jumped up, ran over to him and

174

wrapped him with a blanket. He didn't even know I had done this. He was still saying, "Swaha, swaha, swaha!"

Swamiji performing homa while Shree Maa is in Meditation

Swamiji didn't know what I had done and what happened with the fire until he completed his worship. From sunrise to sunset he had performed the fire ceremony. When he finished, he hurriedly went outside to attend the calls of nature, and people said, "Babaji! Babaji! What happened to your cloth; it's all burnt!" At that time, he became aware of it, and said, "Oh, it's burnt!" He's a sadhu; he doesn't care about himself. He didn't want to break his asana (sitting posture). He was chanting with Mother and he was completely with Mother. His consciousness was at another place, he was with pure consciousness on the subtle plane. He believes, "Whatever Mother gives me, I will accept." He has tremendous will power.

When we were in the mountains, Thakur talked to me while I was in samadhi and said, "You have to go to America to show tapasya." I woke up and said to Swamiji,

"Mother told me that we have to go to America." He said, "You can cut my head off, but I'm not going to America. It's Mahamaya land!"

Three months later, we came down to the plains. At that time, Swamiji had only a twenty day visa for India. We went to get another long-term visa, and they increased it by only twenty more days. Then we went to Calcutta, and we tried to get another long-term visa, but they gave him only a week. They said, "You can't stay in this country anymore, you have to go somewhere else now. Go back to your own country."

So we went to Bangladesh for one month, but when we tried to come back to India, the government wouldn't let him in. He wrote a very persuasive letter to the Indian government, but they said, "You've stayed here for so many years, you've done enough sadhana here, now go back to your country and make it divine!"

But he wouldn't listen! I was completely in another world. Even when Swamiji didn't get his visa, I didn't remember that Ramakrishna told me to come to America. I was in another consciousness. It wasn't until many years later, when we were already living in the U.S., that I remembered what Thakur had said.

RECEIVING GOD'S DARSHAN

Remember when Purnima saw Mother's form and she became unconscious of external reality. When you see a real form of Mother, you become unconscious to the external (world) and become aware of the subtle. At that time you see Her in your subtle consciousness. Purnima was with Mother in her subtle consciousness, and to other people it looked like she fainted. The fact that Purnima's fainting meant that she went to her subtle consciousness

176

and when she came back to her gross consciousness, she started to cry. That happens.

For example, when I first went to the Annapurna Temple in Benares, I saw Mother Annapurna and I fainted. Here is what happened: A big, big light came to me from Mother Annapurna's statue and I lost external consciousness. It felt so beautiful inside me. I was with Mother and She was telling me, "We are One!" We were completely connected. It was so beautiful!

God gives us darshan. Sometimes we know it; sometimes we don't know it. God gives darshan in many ways. Why don't we know sometimes? Because we're not that aware, we're not pure enough to feel it.

One day I was in the Martinez temple and I was standing in the kitchen. At that moment Jyoti looked at me, and she was pure and suddenly she saw me as Kali. She bowed down and said, "Mother, you are Kali. I saw you." But she actually saw very little. For only a moment she was aware of something. If she saw the real form and she went into samadhi, then I would have been really happy! If she was really aware, she would have gone into samadhi like Purnima did. People see according to their own perception.

Some people get a vision if they have faith, some people don't get! It depends on how much faith they have. If they have that faith, they've got it! And God will be really happy about that, really happy.

After Self-realization you become absolutely fearless. You can only be afraid if you think there's something apart from you that threatens you. When you become Self-realized, you see that everything is a part of you. There can't be fear in that state anymore than there can be darkness after sunrise.

TEACHINGS

I have an opportunity to be with Jesus 24 hours a day.
We try to pray through our work by doing it with Jesus,
for Jesus, to Jesus.
That helps us to put our whole heart and soul into doing it.
The dying, the crippled, the mental, the unwanted,
the unloved, they are Jesus in disguise.
I don't claim anything of the work. It's His work.
I'm like a little pencil in His hand. That's all.
He does the thinking. He does the writing.
The pencil has nothing to do it.
The pencil has only to be allowed to be used.
- Mother Teresa from of Calcutta

Like Mother Teresa, Shree Maa sees every one as God and every thing as the creation of God. Interestingly, she views this world as a play and not real. In this interview, she discusses the mysteries of life and death.

Shree Maa:

A higher soul lives with each individual soul that's the theme of this book! (Laughing) You can see how beautiful the Rudrashtadyai is! You are with everybody. If you can see yourself with a higher soul everywhere, it will be so beautiful. You will not be alone; even in the jungle, you will not be alone.

I always see Ramakrishna everywhere, everywhere "Thakur." If anybody came to me, they were sent by Thakur; wherever I went, Thakur was taking me. In that way, I saw that everything is Thakur. (Laughing) Still now, if anybody comes to me, I still see Ramakrishna. Thakur is there even if that person is living in duality.

Remember you have a relation with everything, you have interaction with everything and you're with everything. You are never alone. Your action and reaction are going on constantly with everything. But Maya is so strong; it makes us forget. (Laughing) Fun, huh? We came into this world to play. It is a play! It's completely a play. Just play the game.

I asked Parvati, Shree Maa's devotee in America since a long time, to explain Shree Maa's statement "a higher soul lives with each individual soul and we have relation with everything."

Here is Parvati's explanation:

Recently Shree Maa was describing how her life was centered on God from a very early age. I asked "Isn't that because you were born with God?" She said, "Everybody is!"

I said, "But from your birth you have never felt yourself as separate from God. Isn't that right?"

She said, "Yes, that is true. I grew up with God. When one grows up with God, it is easier to remember God all of the time."

Just as Shree Maa has never considered herself as separate from God, in the same way, she sees all of creation and each one of us as a part of God. By accepting her way, we open the possibility for all of us to experience the same attitude of connectivity with every thing. This has empowered me to keep on growing and changing in many ways, on many levels, for many years.

Someone asked me, "What is the most important thing that you have learned after being with Shree Maa for so many years?"

I would have to say that doing sadhana (spiritual practices of chanting, singing, performing puja, meditating, etc.) is the essence of Maa's teaching. It is through these practices that we gain wisdom and devotion, earn the grace of the Guru, and we remember our true divine nature. We develop inner strength to face life's challenges, and we gain an understanding that we are all connected as one big family. With this understanding we seek to serve our community and make the world a better place. What better example do we have, than our beloved Shree Maa who continues to give and uplift us all?

DUALITY

Shree Maa:

I was totally beyond this world of play and duality when I was in samadhi all the time. My mind did not get pulled to the world; it was always with God. I never asked people, "What is your name? Where are you from? What do you do?" Never! Only since coming to America, I have started to ask people these questions. I was living in a completely different world.

Now this world is extremely different because I'm in consciousness. I talk now; before I did not talk very much. Every once in a while some words came from my mouth, but usually I didn't talk. Now, when I see you, I ask questions, "How are you? How's it going with you?" Before I never talked about these things.

Someday we'll return this five-element body to the earth and then we'll go on our own journey. Yes, it would be a great day. That's the time when you'll go to your home, your real home. (Laughing) You'll be free! It's exactly the same as when we opened the gate of the peacock cage, and then the peacocks were free. They were dancing and happy. In the same way this body is a cage, and the soul is living inside the cage. One day the door will be opened, and you'll be free! Then you're home! This body is not eternal, only the soul is eternal.

When we don't know what reality is, we become sad. Maya makes us sad. But that sadness is also not eternal, it's short-lived.

In the meantime, we have to be good actors, never take it seriously. If you take it seriously, you're living in your head and unconditional love will never come to you. Pure love will never come to you, if you take yourself too seriously. I can't teach you too much, it will have to come from within.

Gautam, another devotee of Shree Maa gives his perspective on what it is like to be with Shree Maa and how it has enabled him to overcome duality. Here is Gautam's expression about his journey of overcoming his duality:

My association with Shree Maa and Swamiji is the catalyst for primarily subduing, then gradually penetrating the bulwarks of the ego's domain. Their weapons include heavy doses of the elixirs (unconditional love and support) which makes the devotee at first intoxicated with love of God: a sense of timelessness, floating along with a no problem attitude and ultimately in sweet oneness with the universe.

Previous to my meeting of Shree Maa and Swamiji in 1985, I was in a quandary: how to find oneness with the Creator. The path I had traveled thus far had given me great inspiration and teachers who revealed methods for sadhana. But I needed more guidance and an in-depth understanding of how to focus on a goal that could change my life. "When we yearn for God with sincere longing, He hears our cry and appears in the form of a True Teacher who will guide us." This is exactly what happened to me one day as I sat with a friend in the cafeteria of an ashram sipping tea. He told me of two saints who had come to America from India without anything except for two suitcases and an enormous amount of pure bhava (intuitive vision). When he asked me if I would like to meet them at his house, I enthusiastically agreed.

The setting for my meeting with my future gurus was what you might call "right out of the Hollywood memorable." The house my friend's father owned had been on the market for sale for 2 to 3 years, but somehow never sold. Later I found out that his mother had been killed in that house, and her soul was still there waiting to be freed. He had invited Mother and Swamiji to come and stay at the house and send the soul on to higher realms. They had been preparing a statue of Kali (Divine Mother in the form of She who takes away our darkness), molding Her from clay, straw, sticks and string. So imagine: you are ringing the door bell, your friend opens the door inviting you into this house with no furniture, Swamiji coming forward to greet

you smiling, with dear Shree Maa standing quietly behind him with folded hands. Then to walk into the washroom and see this image of Kali in the cement laundry sink in process of being made - leaves one breathless.

I was invited to move into the humble house with them after twelve consecutive nights of going there. What a blessing! I started my journey towards feeling connected with the universe; many times of testing, failures, little successes. Thank you, Shree Maa and Swamiji for all that you have given me.

They have always given their best in taming my wild horses of the mind and as gurus they have fearlessly spoken their message of renunciation, discrimination, peace, and love, without assuaging egos. An 'oft-repeated' phrase is worth hearing once more: "the life-changing benefits of seeking out saints and wearing out their doorstep for the sharing of satsangha with them cannot be praised enough!"

This is just one person's story of how meeting with Shree Maa has inspired me to study, practice, become more pure, nurture divinity, overcome my ego, see the light of wisdom, and ultimately (no matter how long it takes) reach that perfect state of oneness with the Creator.

UNIVERSE

Shree Maa:

This universe is big! We're very little. (Laughing) Maybe you will be surprised with this talk. This creation, it's unbelievable. What can one say? Therefore, we say, "Not this, not that." There is nothing to talk about.

This universe has lots of planets. One doesn't just have to stay only on one planet. It depends on what kind of karma we are doing. If we do good karma, we go to other places and stay there. On some planets there is no night, only day. On some planets nobody dies; you're eternal. The bodies on these planets are more subtle than ours. One can change into any form!

This universe is so big and there are so many things in it. When you do sadhana and speak the truth and respect your actions, you'll know who you are and you'll know the whole universe. The whole universe is you and everybody is your family. Therefore we teach you to respect your actions and then you'll know what you are here to do. That's why we are trying to cure your lifetime karma with sadhana.

When pure love is there, we are one soul. Nobody can go anywhere. When you have pure love, you are with everybody. You'll get lovey-dovey with the whole creation. Soon the feelings of universality will dissolve because you have to come down again to do karma yoga, to unite through your every action.

ANGELS

Shree Maa:

Angel means a form of Godliness. In the West we think of Gods and Goddesses as angels, while in India we call the Goddesses as Kali or Durga. It's just a different perception and a different name.

Someone recently told me about this movie Patch Adams. Patch was a doctor and he had a female friend who loved butterflies. She was killed by a crazy man, who then killed himself. Patch was so sad when she died that he wanted to resign from the world. He went to a mountain and was talking to God, and then a butterfly came and sat down on his heart. He felt God had come to him in the form of a butterfly and he went back to work.

When one gets higher consciousness, one can see these things. When one goes deeper and deeper into self, one can see and know everything. One realizes you are related with everything.

Many people have first hand experience of Shree Maa's highly evolved intuitive abilities where she seemingly sees and knows every thing. I asked Abha, a doctor who looks after Shree Maa's health to share her perspective.

Here is Abha:

I met Shree Maa and Swamiji in 1986 when my husband was renting our house in Concord. What strikes me now is how coolly that transaction, startlingly brief and matter-of-fact, was conducted. In sharp contrast, today, 22 years later, I hang on to each and every moment I can spend with Shree Maa whenever I meet her. Like an eager child, I am unashamed to take advantage of my job as a physician so that I can enquire about her health, converse with her for longer, and become more involved with her. I do not know when this transition from business to infatuation and devotion occurred, but I am ecstatic to be in this state.

I have always believed in God. However, my faith was perhaps more a result of being born and raised in a religious family than a true personal decision. As an adult, prior to meeting Shree Maa, I would sometimes wonder if God was fact or fiction.

However, my involvement with Shree Maa has transformed my faith, particularly through the repeated occurrence of miraculous events that are neither logical nor scientific. One might call them coincidences, except these are not rare or random events, happening far too often to be mere chance.

One such incidence regarding my brother's relationship with Shree Maa comes immediately to mind when I think of such "coincidences." My brother, who lives overseas, is Shree Maa's devotee, and so it was natural that when I met Shree Maa each weekend, she would enquire about him and his family. One day, in addition to her regular questions, she very pointedly asked me to tell him that she loved him very much. That evening, I called him up to convey her message. After several moments of stunned silence, my brother revealed that a few days ago, while thinking about Shree Maa, he specifically wondered if she still loved him. However, he had not confided these thoughts to Shree Maa or anyone; how she knew to reassure him of her love is inexplicable by regular logic and convention.

Even I have personally experienced Shree Maa's "coincidences." Once, while cleaning the temple, my shirt caught fire and I sustained a second degree burn on my side. The episode took only a few minutes, but I felt immense helplessness and agony. Shree Maa was in her house at that time, felt uneasy and called on the kitchen phone to check if every thing was alright. Upon hearing the news, she came immediately, armed with medical supplies. Apparently, a few days earlier, she had had a premonition about a potential mishap with fire.

During my recovery, Shree Maa called regularly. In these tender, maternal conversations, she mentioned that my father (who passed away seven years ago) wanted her to look after me.

How can we explain the communication channels through which Shree Maa's premonition, her sense of uneasiness, and her knowledge of my father's wishes from beyond the grave, so to speak, traveled? Simply put: we cannot. All that I can say assuredly is that, thanks to Shree Maa's living example, I now believe there is a fourth dimension and I now know, beyond a shade of doubt, that God exists. On weekends when I visit the Devi Mandir, I am fortunate to have the opportunity to walk with Shree Maa and discuss matters related to the health of her gross body, while Shree Maa, in her far more powerful brand of medicine, diagnoses and heals my spirit, enabling my soul to walk a little farther on this path towards eternal bliss.

DHARMA

Shree Maa:

There is always dharma (a righteous path) and adharma (opposite of dharma). Ultimately adharma is erased and Truth always wins.

Ram came to earth and destroyed all adharma. Ravana chose to come to this world, and he chose his karma so he would realize himself quickly. He had ego, he lived with ego, but ultimately he dissolved his ego. I told you how he cut off nine of his heads because he was a great Shiva devotee. This happened before he came down to earth as Ram's enemy. There's more to Ravana's story[9].

Every action is taking us towards God or towards worldliness, towards unity or sesparation. It's wise to take the good and bad away, and just realize it's all God. Some people will use their suffering to become true and get free while others may not. If you're conscious, you will realize God.

Neelima describes how she realized both worldliness and Godliness through Shree Maa's blessings:

I was in San Francisco in August 1990, on my way to New York for an IVF procedure when my brother-in-law took me to meet his Guru. I vividly remember my first meeting with Shree Maa; she was statuesque, clad in white with her serene face framed by long hair. The love and humility with which Shree Maa and Swamiji interacted with all was awe inspiring. Shree Maa did not speak many words and neither did Swamiji give any sermons, but so many questions seemed to have got answered by merely being in their proximity.

I asked for a blessing, she blessed me with a *rudraksh.* Instantly, all my anxieties dissolved and I felt reassured that my visit to New York will be successful. I soon learned that the first IVF procedure was successful. After eight months, I gave birth to healthy twin boys and blissful motherhood

---

9 Refer to the reference section for Ravana's story.

kept me totally occupied for many years without any direct contact with Shree Maa.

In the mid 90s, Shree Maa visited India and stayed at my father-in-law's house. When during the evening puja she put a sandal paste mark on my husband's forehead, Sanjay, my husband, (who had little interest or faith in religion or spiritual practices) felt a wonderful sensation which he had not experienced before. Sanjay was intrigued and I was grateful for Shree Maa's second blessing. The next day Shree Maa and Swamiji left for Varanasi.

Sanjay and I could not help ourselves but to follow her. We both have visited Varanasi numerous times before and frankly we were not really enamored by the city. Unlike any previous visit, this trip with Shree Maa was deeply mystical - walking through the narrow lanes, in and out of temples, taking the boat ride on the *Ganga*, trying to keep up with Shree Maa as she raced up the steep steps to visit Trailang Swami's Ashram and participating in the *homas* performed by Swamiji. While our bodies got tired, our souls soared and our minds quieted down. This magical experience opened our eyes and hearts to the essence of this eternal city of our births.

I consider Shree Maa as my mother, my guru and a living Goddess. Shree Maa has taught me so much - the highs are God's grace and the lows teach precious lessons which could not have been learned any other way. Ever since my first meeting with Shree Maa it has become clear to me that in her presence obstacles dissolve and doubts disappear. As I stumble along on this journey of life, I feel assured knowing that she is always there watching over me, guiding me firmly and patiently towards life's ultimate goal – be simple, be true and be free.

BE TRUE. Say what you mean and do what you say. If you are true, you will be without fear. If your conscience is clear, your heart will be silent. That is Peace. No matter what the result.

BE SIMPLE. Many words are a burden to the soul. The real message of your heart will be communicated by your actions. The words will only explain the actions. But they must agree, lest we become hypocrites, who preach what we ourselves do not practice.

BE FREE. Leave your selfishness behind. The people whose opinions are valued will love us for what we are, not for what we have. The respect which can be bought is as useless as a tree which bears neither flowers nor fruits. When the leaves will fall and the trunk wither, none will come again.

TAKE REFUGE IN GOD. Neither your friends, relations, nor others will take you to heaven. Only Wisdom will be our salvation.

CULTIVATE WISDOM. Learn from everyone, everywhere. Then use that knowledge which will bring you into harmony with the universe.

DEVELOP DISCRIMINATION. Pursue only those desires which will make you free. Leave the ones which will get you into trouble. Know the difference and remind yourself daily. Remember that the God you seek resides in every atom. You can offer respect to every atom, even while you maintain your own discipline inside. That you are a spiritual seeker is not something you need to show outside. It will manifest in your behavior, without your having to try. If we are gentle, loving, kind and honest in our dealings, that is spiritual. Your spirituality cannot be hidden. Similarly, if one is full of fears and trying to hide his inner emotions, such a person is not full of spirit. That is only ego.

LET ALL OUR ACTIONS MANIFEST OUR LOVE. Work is visible love, the expression of love that we can see. People want realization, liberation, to become enlightened. Do not think it is something different from doing for others as you would have them do for you.

SPIRITUALITY IS VERY SIMPLE. "I am everywhere," says the sage. "I exist in every form of creation. If I hurt any form, I hurt myself. If raise any form to a higher level, I myself, find progress." It is easy.

Shree Maa's Music stirs the soul

DUALITY

Shree Maa:

There has always been duality and fighting, "Us against them, light against darkness." As long as there are two poles, then there's tension in the middle. Whenever you have one side, you create the other side. In the history of humanity it has always been this way. The only way out is to stay in the center (the witness) and watch the whole thing.

How does one stay in the center and watch the whole thing? Here is Bhuvananda's suggestion:

Shree Maa's life has no duality. It is an expression of purity, a divine being who is one with God. I see this everyday in her worship and in her caring for her spiritual children, while she remains completely free of egotism and attachment. Without her example, how can we attempt to conquer our own egos? Her great love of the Chandi has inspired me to make its recitation my primary spiritual practice, so that I might be able to go deeper inside myself.

KARMA

Shree Maa:

If you are doing good karma this lifetime, next lifetime you'll be born as a higher soul than this lifetime, and with good karma. In a similar way, Nature can sometimes be lower, sometimes higher. It depends on what kind of desires we have, like in that story about the sadhu who was doing sadhana in the jungle. He fell in love with a deer and was doing seva to the deer with love and attachment. In his next life he was born as a deer. Do you understand?

Everything is attachment. If you're attached to good karma, you'll get good karma next lifetime!

But one thing always remember, when you're trying to purify yourself, and your mind gets caught with negative impurities, always try to cure that. For example, if your mind is going to negative things, right away say the Gayatri mantra. Right away! If any bad thought comes to you, always correct it with Gayatri mantra. Any mantra! That's called prayaschitta, curing all negative thoughts. That way you will be safe and not perpetuating the thought. If you don't correct it, you're creating karma (thoughts also create karma not just actions). Be careful all the time, karma is subtle.

There are four kinds of karma in existence: first Samkshipta is the karma which is completed, over and done with; second, Vartmana is the present karma, which is going on right now; third, Prarabdha are the actions which were begun in the past and which will come to fruition in the future; and fourth is Nityakarma which is eternal. Buddhists and Hindus believe that all births take place in order to finish karma. We are all bound by unfinished karma.

Every being manifested and every moment that comes to birth, comes because of our unfinished business.

One can achieve realization in one lifetime. One can be born again and forget some of the realized wisdom from a previous life. When you're born again, at a certain time the wisdom comes back or you can be born with it. It depends on what karma you are doing in this lifetime. This is not one lifetime, nor is this a lifetime after a previous lifetime - this is one life, just one life!

This connection with everything is a very beautiful relationship. When you realize that this universe is so beautiful, you will say, "Brahma, Brahma, Brahma, God, God, God!"

Swamiji worships Shree Maa as a way of life

How could a human's worth ever be such?
And God Knowing all our thoughts
and all our thoughts are innocent steps
on the path
then addressed my heart,
God revealed a sublime truth to the world,
when He sang.
"I am made whole by your life.
Each soul, each soul completes me."
-Hafiz

SHE IS THE ONE

Bill Fetzer shares how he met Shree Maa and how their relationship changed his life. Bill Fetzer:

This is not just a story, it is a soul awakened to the light. This really happened. This is not a parable, or the story of a long dead Rishi and their disciple. This is real life today.

What will it take for all of us to have that awakening? Nothing more than surrendering heart and mind to realized beings and following their advice.

For many years I taught Transcendental Meditation in Philadelphia, Pennsylvania, while raising a family. When our Guru asked Americans to move to Iowa to meditate together to help create world peace, my wife and I and our children answered the call. For many years we followed a routine of meditation and work in the world, giving our best to help make this world a better place.

After some time, I felt a void in my heart. I needed to have a personal and direct relationship with my Guru. I had read in the books of the lives of great saints and intuitively knew that the only way to find God was thru the grace of a God Realized Master. Time passed, and I met many saints and teachers. At each meeting I hoped to meet my Master, but my heart never sang out, "THIS IS THE ONE".

One day, in 1997, our mailman, told me a woman saint, Shree Maa was coming to a city near ours. She was featured in a book by Linda Johnson called: "Woman Saints of India." I immediately purchased the book, and read about her. Her story fascinated me, and I wanted to meet her. On the day of the meeting, while eating lunch, a bright yellow thunderbolt pulsed thru my head. I shouted out: "What was that?" startling my wife and 9 year old son. Who could say what it was: a message? A sign? My imagination?

We drove towards the meeting hall on the campus of the University of Iowa, the excitement growing. When we entered the hall, we saw about 100 folks of all ages standing and clapping to strange yet joyful songs. With huge smiles on their faces, they danced in place and looked to the front of the room. The music came from a small group sitting on the floor. In the center was a small woman, wrapped in a beautiful bright yellow sari. Next to her was a white man, dressed in Indian clothes. While I could not understand the words she sang, I could feel the electricity in the air. My heart opened. She sang, we danced - we had no choice.

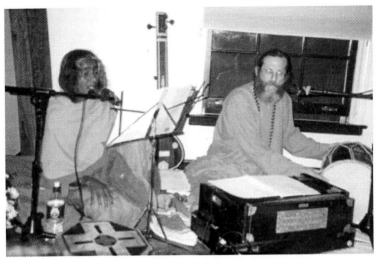

Shree Maa and Swamiji singing

Suddenly the music stopped. In the golden silence, a line formed and one by one, each person knelt down in front of Shree Maa and received a big red dot on their third eye, and a piece of candy in their hand. Some mumbled a quiet "thank you" to her, most of us just smiled into her beautiful eyes.

When she left the hall, folks began to clean up and I joined in. It was the least I could do. No one had asked for money, and yet I knew the hall was not free and they had traveled from out of town. I just wanted to give something back. As we worked I asked one of her devotees about her and her mission. He said that she was a disciple of Ramakrishna, a 19th century saint from Calcutta. "Who is that?" I asked. "What did he teach?"

195

He was recognized in his time as a great saint, he said. Some even said he was an avatar. He taught that all religions were equal in the eyes of God, and that all lead to the same goal and that everyone should be free to practice their faith. Shree Maa is traveling the United States at his request, visiting her children, and "waking them up" and inspiring them to remember their true nature.

"At his request?" I asked. How can someone no longer in a body provide guidance? He is with her always, and speaks to her in the silence of deep meditation. Well, I thought to myself, this is something new. A 19th century saint who taught religious tolerance sending his 20th century Indian disciple around America to "wake up" and inspire her children.

As we cleaned up, I wondered when I could see Shree Maa again? Just then, someone said they would be traveling to Fairfield, my hometown, for satsangha. They would be staying at the home of my friend, the mailman. His home, with a beautiful Temple inside, was called, "Deva Loka, or Home of the Goddess." Wonder of wonders; she was coming to Fairfield. I wondered if she was THE ONE?

I hardly slept that night, and called my friend and asked if I could help arrange his home for their visit. He said there was much to do and he needed help. With a great flurry of activity, we readied the home and Temple for her arrival. When she arrived, I watched from a distance, too much in awe of her to approach and say hello. After she settled in, she toured the property and when she saw the old barn, mostly filled with huge bales of hay, she said she wanted it arranged so the sacred fire ceremony could be held there.

We all looked at each other. How to arrange huge flammable hay bales in order to accommodate a fire ceremony? She said to move them to the rear of the barn and stack them so they could be used as bleachers for the crowd to sit upon. What a novel idea, we said, and we set about transforming the barn into a Divine Temple, fit for the Divine Fire.

Never did we think about the task of moving huge heavy hay bales around. We just set upon them, heaving them about. To this day I marvel that we performed the task. I was filled with an energy that I had never felt before. Could she be THE ONE?

Now she said, we will experience the Divine Fire. For the first time, I was drawn to Swamiji: this middle aged white man, dressed in orange Indian clothes, followed Shree Maa like a shadow. He sat down in front of the metal fire pit, behind him wood was stacked high. Shree Maa sat next to him and closed her eyes. With a commanding yet loving voice, he began to sing sacred mantras and placed flowers inside the fire pit. In silence, we watched, entranced, as he chanted. When he lit the fire, we all gasped. It was as if a living being had entered the fire pit. The fire was alive, and the flames danced and jumped with the joy of being in Shree Maa and Swamiji's presence.

Shree Maa and Swamiji performing homa in Fairfield

Then Swamiji instructed us to take up our bowls of rice, and taught us a mantra, Om Gam Ganapataye Swaha, inviting Lord Ganesh to come to the fire and bless our ceremony. Then in unison, 200 hands dipped into bowls of rice, and offered it into the fire while saying the mantra. It was amazing. As we completed one, he taught us another, and another, until the barn was ringing with the sound of unified voices calling upon the Gods and Goddesses to accept our love, and our karma, and send it all to the highest heaven. Swamiji called it a karma barbecue. We roared with laughter. Nothing like this had ever come to town.

When the fire ceremony was complete, Shree Maa said we should perform arati. She lit the sacred lights, and instructed us on how to offer our inner light to the light of the Divine fire. She and Swamiji and her devotees played their instruments and sang, while we took turns offering the sacred light, and clapping and dancing. As the singing grew louder and the energy grew higher, I started to dance like a whirling dervish, out of control, next to the fire. Suddenly hands grabbed me and pulled me back from the fire, and I realized I had almost jumped into it.

When the song ended, I heard a devotee say: "Hey, come here." I looked up at the fire and saw him motioning to someone to come to the front. I looked around to see who they wanted, and everyone was looking at me. Shree Maa wanted me to come up front. "Me? You want me?" I asked. "Yes" He said, Shree Maa wants you to come up front.

I walked thru the crowd to the front by the fire, and Shree Maa motioned to me to come around the fire and sit next to her. Stunned, I obeyed. I sat down next to her, and she handed me a tambourine. Well, that stunned me to the core of my being. I had no sense of time, and could not keep a rhythm to save my life, and here She was asking me to play this instrument with her and the band. So the band began, and I played along keeping perfect time. Needless to say, I wondered, IS SHE THE ONE?

Shree Maa serene and blissful as always

The next morning, Friday, Shree Maa was leaving. When I awoke on Friday morning, I was filled with dread, a deep pain in my heart unlike anything I had ever felt before. She was leaving, how would I live without her? What was I to do? I have a family and a life, I can't go running after her. I wanted to calm down so I could see her before she left. I sat up in bed and meditated.

As I began to meditate, a strange thing happened. Pictures began to appear in my mind like a movie. It started from when I was born and showed scenes from every stage of my life. As each scene unfolded and melted into the next, I saw Shree Maa standing and watching over me. She was my guardian angel, my Guru, silently guiding and protecting me, through thick and thin, good and bad. She was ever present.

I started to cry. From the depths of my being, emotions welled up and I cried. I cried with joy because She was always with me, and then I cried with shame, because She saw me at my worst, and I cried louder because She did not judge, She only gave Divine Love to me, always. Then, the movie went back in time, and I saw myself in another form, as an adult, dressed in orange cloth, walking with a staff, with Her, and sitting at a Divine Fire ceremony. Out of the silence of the movie, Her voice welled up, a soft whisper at first, then louder and louder, repeating the same thing over and over: "I came back for you."

Meanwhile, my wife heard me crying and came to comfort me. I could only say to her, "I must get to Shree Maa. Please help me." She helped me dress, and bundled me into the car. She drove while I sat in a daze. My mind was trying to figure out if it had been a dream or some wild fantasy? What is happening to me? We arrived at the home and went inside. Everyone was sitting on the floor, eating breakfast. Someone asked if I was hungry, and placed a bowl of oatmeal in front of me. How could I eat? I just wanted to talk to Shree Maa. As if reading my mind, She arose from the floor, and walked to the other side of the room. I quickly jumped up and pulling my wife after me, walked over to Her. Now standing face to face, She said: "I came back for you."

Well, that settled it: SHE IS THE ONE.

Referenced Stories

(1) One day two kings who were brothers were out hunting near the Nilaparvata Mountain and they got really thirsty. There was no water anywhere. They walked for a long time until they were deep in the jungle.

Then they saw an old lady walking with a stick. She said, "Oh, are you thirsty? Go this way, and you can get water." They went there and saw a little pond near where the Kamakhya Temple now stands. When they drank the water, the older king's ring suddenly fell into the pond. The king thought, "This is very strange. She must be a ghost. Let's get out of here!" And they ran away and found their way back to their kingdom.

One day the same two brothers went to Benares, the holiest city in India. Before the trip, the Divine Mother appeared to the younger brother in a dream and asked, "When will you make a temple for me?" The younger brother was so happy to get the Mother's darshan that he ran to his older brother and said, "Brother! Mother came to me in a dream and told me to make a temple!" The older brother dismissed him, "It was just a dream. Forget about it!"

One day the older brother was walking in Benares to the Vishvanath Temple, the holiest temple in Benares, and he was shocked to see the same lady with the stick that he saw in the jungle. She was laughing! He got really scared. He said to himself, "I'll kill her! This is a ghost!" You see, first the Divine Mother appeared to the younger brother in a dream and now she was appearing in another form to the older brother.

He went behind her with his sword drawn so he could kill her, but she got away. The king's soldiers tried to help capture her, but she went this way and that way and escaped. Nobody could catch her! Ultimately, she went inside the Annapurna Temple, although it was closed. Just before she went inside, she gave the ring back to the king saying, "I am not a ghost! I am Mother."

The two kings came back from Benares to their kingdom. The younger brother said, "We have to make a temple. Mother said when we build the temple, we must put a little gold into each brick." The elder brother said, "You're crazy!"

The elder brother's wife believed the younger brother and she had lots of gold. She gave the gold to the younger brother and they started to build the Kamakhya Temple, but the contractor took a lot of the gold, instead of putting it into the bricks. They finished the building, but it fell down because the contractor cheated.

Mother came in a dream and told the younger brother how he had been cheated. After that, they rebuilt the building, but this time every brick had a little gold in it.

(2) One day I was torn with intolerable anguish. My heart seemed to be wrung as a damp cloth might be wrung...I was racked with pain. A terrible frenzy seized me at the thought that I might never be granted the blessing of this Divine vision. I thought if that were so, then enough of this life! A sword was hanging in the sanctuary of Kali. My eyes fell upon it and an idea flashed through my brain like a flash of lightning. "The sword! It will help me to end it." I rushed up to it, and seized it like a madman ... And lo! The whole scene, doors, windows, the temple itself vanished ... It seemed as if nothing existed any more. Instead I saw an ocean of the Spirit, boundless, dazzling. In whatever direction I turned, great luminous waves were rising. They bore down upon me with a loud roar, as if to swallow me up. In an instant they were upon me. They broke over me;

they engulfed me. I was suffocated. I lost consciousness and I fell... How I passed that day and the next I know not. Round me rolled an ocean of ineffable joy. And in the depths of my being I was conscious of the presence of the Divine Mother.

(3) In Ravana's kingdom, the Shiva lingam (a symbol of Shiva used for worship) went down below the ground. Ravana's mother said to him, "This kingdom will be dissolved because Shiva is not happy and he went under the earth. Please go to Shiva and pray to him and bring his symbol for worship back." Ravana said, "Yes, I'll do that. Lord Shiva will listen to me."

So Ravana went to Kailash (Shiva's home in the Himalayas) and Shiva wasn't there. Shiva knew Ravana was coming. Ravana sang so many stotrams and prayers, but still Shiva didn't appear. Then Ravana did a homa (fire ceremony) and still Shiva didn't come. Then Ravana said, "Okay, if you aren't giving darshan, I'll dissolve myself. I'll give my head to you." Ravana had ten heads and one by one he cut off his heads and threw them into the fire. When he was about to cut off the last head, Shiva appeared.

(5) In front of the Master was an artistically decorated low wooden seat for the deity, though no image had been brought. Now Mother (Sarada Devi) entered the room and looked intently as the worship proceeded. After the chanting of the appropriate mantras he beckoned Sarada to the decorated seat. She had become semi-conscious through spiritual fervor as she had been watching the worship, and now, not knowing what she was doing, she moved forward as though under a charm, and sat on the allotted low stool facing the Master.

The Master took some sanctified water from the pitcher and sprinkled it on her body. Then he mentally identified the different limbs of the Holy Mother with the corresponding parts of the deity and considering her as none other than the Deity Herself, worshiped her duly with the usual sixteen kinds of offering.

By and by, the Mother lost all outer consciousness and the worshiper, too, gradually lost himself in beatitude.

from *Holy Mother* by Swami Gambhirananda

(6) One evening a British officer, whose wife was seriously ill in England, visited Goraknath at his ashram in Nepal. The doctors were saying his wife wouldn't live. That night Goraknath went to England in his subtle body to save her. He visited the officer's wife and healed her, but nobody knew.

One month later, the British officer's wife came back to Nepal and she was healthy. She visited Goraknath with her husband and when she saw him she said, "He saved me! He is the one who came to me one night and cured me!" Later they found it was the same night her husband had visited Goraknath. It's beautiful! You can go anywhere, you can make your form anywhere, when you are completely pure. It's so beautiful, I cannot express this to you!

(7) Trailinga Swami was in Nepal, staying near the famous Shiva temple called Pashupati Nath. The Nepalese king's daughter hadn't gotten married and she was getting old. It was hard for the Nepalese king who thought, "What should I do? I would give my daughter's hand in marriage to anybody at this point." He was losing patience.

Meanwhile, the princess had decided to perform a puja to Shiva to get married. Accompanied by a guard of soldiers, she went to the Pashupati Nath Temple to do this puja and brought lots of garlands and other puja items.

Trailinga Swami was sitting there naked; he was always naked. He said to the princess, "Give me your garland!" She got mad! He was sitting naked with all these beggars and she was offended. There she was in the temple to do worship and this beggar was disturbing her. She couldn't control her anger!

After that, she did the puja, and when she was coming out of the temple, she saw the same garland on Trailinga Swami that she had just put on Shiva! She got even more mad! She said, "This man went behind me and took my garland that I offered to the deity!" So she went back into the temple to see Shiva and she saw that the garland she had placed on Shiva was still there! Again she came back out and saw that Trailinga Swami was wearing the same garland. She did this three times and by that time she was so mad she said, "I'm sending soldiers to arrest you because you stole my garland!" She didn't know it was Trailinga Swami. Trailinga Swami said, "Go home! You will find your husband there."

She went home and she saw that what he said was true. A prince from another state had come to marry her. You can see how beautiful Trailinga was. He took the garland using another form to maintain a divine relationship with the princess.

She told the king what had happened and the king said, "Oh, that must be Trailinga Swami," because he knew Trailinga Swami from when the lion sat on Trailinga's lap in the jungle.

(8) One day two sadhus were going by the thief's house. They had nothing; one jhola (bag) and one common bowl. When the thief caught the two sadhus, he was going

to kill them, but one of them said, "Why are you killing people? You're creating bad karma." The gunda said, "I'm not creating bad karma, I'm taking care of my family! It's my duty! Who will give them food? Give everything you have to me right now!" One of the sadhus said, "Okay, but listen to my question first, and then give an answer. After that you can kill us. Tie us to the tree, go to your house and ask your parents, "I am stealing and killing people in order to support you. Will you share responsibility with me for those actions as you share the food?"

So the gunda agreed and tied them to the tree. He went home and asked his parents, "I am robbing and killing people in order to support you. Will you take a share of my sins as you share in the food?" And his parents said, "Why? Why would we take your sins? You are doing your own karma. You're duty is to take care of us. Every individual takes care of his or her own karma. No, we won't take a share your sins." "Aaah!" said the gunda.

He went to his wife and asked the same question, and his wife said the same thing. And he thought, "Oh, my God. I am taking care of my family with devotion, but they won't take a share of the sins of my karma!"

He returned to see the sadhus and said, "No, they won't take a share of my sins!" The sadhus said, "Then why are you doing these things?" At that time he felt, "Yes, what am I doing?" The sadhus said, "Everybody is responsible for his or her own karma. Do good karma." The gunda asked the sadhus, "How can I be free from all the bad karma I have accumulated?"

The sadhus replied, "Say the name of Rama." The gunda wasn't pure enough to say the name of Rama so the sadhus said, "Say Mara (dead body)." He was really touched, and went into the jungle and started to chant. As he chanted Mara, Mara, Mara it turned into Rama, Rama,

Rama. (Laughing) One day he became a big Rama devotee and he wrote the Ramayana. (The story of Rama, Sita and Hanuman is one of the most loved books in India.)

(9) When Ravana cut off his heads, Shiva was pleased with his devotion and gave him a lingam to take back to his kingdom. But Shiva was also aware that Ravana had too much ego, so he told Ravana that on his way back he should not let the lingam touch the ground.

On the way home, Ravana had to make pooh very badly. He couldn't control it and he had to stop his journey to attend the calls of nature. He asked a young cow herder to hold the Shiva lingam while he was performing his duty and to make sure not put it on the ground. The little boy found the Shiva lingam heavy at first and it became heavier and heavier. The bioy kept calling for Ravana to come back, but he was busy and couldn't return. When the boy couldn't hold the Shiva lingam any more, it fell to the ground and the boy ran away.

When Ravana finally came back he said, "Hai Shiva! What has happened?" He tried to lift the lingam off the ground, but it wouldn't move. Ravana's ego popped out and he said to Shiva, "So you are testing me! Well, if you don't want to come to my kingdom, then fine. One day you'll have to come to me." That Shiva lingam became the jyoti lingam at Baidyanath. Ravana went home empty handed and told his mother, "Shiva has too much pride and he won't come back to our kingdom."

On a subtle level you'll see another story behind this one. Narada was a Rishi who did great tapasya and said that he had become a Brahmagyani (Knower of Universal Truth). He was always saying, "Aham Brahmashmi" (I am God).

One day, Narada asked Vishnu, "What is Maya and what is love?" Vishnu said, "Do tapasya and you will see." During Narada's tapasya he conquered Wind, Rain, and Fire, even Indra, the King of the Gods. He thought, "Aham Brahmashmi, I have conquered everything. I have attained the highest."

Then he went to Shiva, who he loved, and bowed down to Him. He told Shiva, "Aham Brahmashmi, I am the Supreme Divinity." Shiva thought, "Oh, ego. He is bound by illusion."

Shiva said, "Okay, you have become the Supreme Divinity, but don't tell that to Vishnu. Be quiet." Narada said, "Okay Shiva, I won't say anything."

Then Narada went to get Vishnu's darshan because Vishnu was his guru. He didn't listen to Shiva, but kept saying, "Aham Brahmashmi, Aham Brahmashmi, I am God." Vishnu thought, "Oh, he is really full of ego right now. I will send him to earth to see how long he can remain the Supreme Divinity."

Vishnu told Narada, "Go to earth and teach your Aham Brahmashmi there." Narada went to earth and Vishnu also went down as a young girl, the daughter of a king. Narada met the girl and they fell in love. Vishnu was playing maya. The girl, the king's daughter, was to pick her husband the next day. Narada went to the king for his daughter's hand and the king told him to come to the ceremony the following day.

Narada was so happy. He went to Vishnu and said, "I fell in love with a king's daughter, who is to be married tomorrow. Vishnu, please make me into the most handsome prince so that the princess will choose me as her husband."

Vishnu said, "Your love is universal, unattached love. This is some other love, this is different. Go tomorrow and I will make you into the most distinctive appearance so you can realize your dreams." So saying, Vishnu gave Narada the face of a monkey.

Many kings and princes came to the ceremony where the princess was to choose her husband. She had a garland that she would put around the head of her new husband. When Narada came, she saw he had a monkey face so she didn't choose him. Instead she gave the garland to Vishnu who had also come in disguise. (Vishnu takes the part of both the bride and the groom because He is all pervading consciousness). When the princess put the garland on Vishnu, Narada got very mad.

Shiva had two disciples, Shringi and Bringi, and Shiva told them to go to the earth to help break Narada's ego. Then Shringi and Bringi showed Narada his face in the water. Narada saw the monkey face and realized what Shiva and Vishnu had done. He said, "Vishnu you tricked me. I'm giving you a curse. You will have to go to the earth and suffer separation from your wife. Shringi and Bringi you have to go too and become demons." Vishnu said, "I agree."

When Shringi and Bringi heard this, they went to Vishnu and asked "What should we do?" Vishnu said, "You have to decide what kind of birth you want to take. If you take an asura (duality) form as demons, you won't have to stay long and you'll come back to heaven sooner." They decided to become asuras so they wouldn't spend a long time on earth. Vishnu became Rama and Shringi and Bringi became Ravana and his brother Kumbakarna.

But when Narada realized he cursed Vishnu, he thought, "What did I do?" and he went to Vishnu and started crying and said, "Vishnu, please forgive me." Vishnu said, "You didn't do anything, this is what I did with you because I need to go to the earth to purify it. You are just the instrument to make that happen."

(*) Swamiji couldn't follow Shree Maa when she left his ashram because he had already made a sankalpa, a spiritual vow, to finish his sadhana, which required several more weeks of chanting. Nobody in the nearby village knew Shree Maa's name or where she came from, so he did not know how to find her. Having completed his sankalpa, Swamiji took the train to Calcutta en route to Gauhati, where he wanted to worship at the Kamakhya Temple. When he arrived in Calcutta, he got down from the train at Dakshineshwar and went straight to Ramakrishna's room, where he sat in a long ecstatic meditation. In his meditation he heard the word "Belgachia," and he went outside and asked someone in Hindi, "What is the meaning of Belgachia?"

The man replied, "Fruit tree." That didn't mean anything to Swamiji so he asked another man, "Do you know of any special fruit trees by that name?"

"No," replied the man, "But there is a bus stop with that name."

Swamiji thanked him and immediately went to the bus stand. "I would like a ticket to Belgachia," he said.

"Which one?" replied the ticket collector. "There are two Belgachias. One is on this side of the river, and the other is on that side."

"I want a ticket on this side of the river," replied Swamiji.

The collector responded, "The stop is over there. The bus just left. The next one will be here in about an hour."

"Where is the bus for the other side of the river?" Swamiji asked. "It's over there," he replied pointing. "They are just boarding."

Swamiji bought a ticket and got on the bus. When he got off the bus at the Belgachia stop a few rickshaw wallahs came over and asked him where he wanted to go.

Not really knowing how to answer, Swamiji said, "Where is Maa?" "Maa is everywhere!" one of them said. Then he called over one of the youngest drivers and said, "You've got a great fare here. Take him on a tour of the city, and show him a temple of Kali."

After touring the town, the rickshaw wallah took Swamiji to the farthest edge of the community to a tiny Kali temple, far away from the main bazaar, and there he stopped.

Swamiji said to him, "Please wait here."

Inside the temple was a small statue of Kali. The pujari appeared astounded to see him, and immediately gave Swamiji a blessing and then said, "May I ask you a question? This is the most amazing thing. All of the foreigners who come to Calcutta go to Belur Math, Dakshineshwar or the Kali Ghat. How did you happen to come to this temple? You are the first foreigner ever to come here."

"I am looking for Maa," Swamiji replied.

"Do you mean Shree Maa? She is in that house across the street," the pujari said pointing. So Swamiji went across the street and knocked on the door of the house where Shree Maa was staying.

When asked to write about our dear Shree Maa, words do not come to mind. Our eyes close, our heart fills with copious amounts of joy and love that can only be expressed through ACTION. Words, phrases and expressions do not provide nearly the infinite amount of justice that Shree Maa deserves. When pressed hard to put words to paper about Shree Maa, the only manifestation that rears above the surface of love is once again ACTION. In our meager viewpoint, we believe that every single moment of every day we are here on this planet is Mother's Day, Her Day. We need to listen to Her messages, mimic Her every action through our every action and strive to honor Her presence by ACTING purely devoted to what-ever degree possible in our continuous existence.

- Sonia & Tania